CHOSEN FOR LEADER·SHIP

SKETCHES OF 39 PRESIDENTS OF THE SOUTHERN BAPTIST CONVENTION

Porter Routh

Broadman Press
Nashville, Tennessee

4265-29

ISBN: 0-8054-6529-4

Subject Headings: BAPTISTS-BIOGRAPHY//SOUTHERN BAPTIST
CONVENTION-BIOGRAPHY

Dewey Decimal Classification: 920

Library of Congress Catalog Card Number: 76-14632

Printed in the United States of America

Contents

INTRODUCTION

Since 1845, when the Southern Baptist Convention was organized in Augusta, Georgia, thirty-nine men have been chosen for leadership as president by the Southern Baptist Convention.

The smallest number of messengers to elect a president were the 124 who elected R. B. C. Howell of Virginia at the meeting in Nashville, Tennessee, in 1851. The largest number of messengers to elect a president were the 18,190 who elected Owen Cooper of Mississippi in Dallas, Texas, in 1974.

Seven of the presidents have been laymen. Five have been seminary presidents. Three have been men who served as governors of their states. One president was a congressman at the time of his election. J. B. Gambrell of Texas was editor of a secular newspaper. Joshua Levering of Maryland was a candidate for president of the United States on the Prohibition ticket. P. H. Mell of Georgia served for fifteen years, the longest term. Two men, F. F. Brown of Tennessee and K. Owen White of Texas, served only one year.

Since the Southern Baptist Convention was organized in 1845, the president has been an ex officio member of the boards of the Convention. He has been a member of the Executive Committee since it was organized in 1917.

Primarily, the president serves as a presiding officer, but he is chosen for leadership. He does not speak *for* Southern Baptists, but he often has a chance to speak *to* Southern

Baptists in general meetings and through various media.

It has been my good fortune to work closely with the fifteen men who have served since the time of Pat Neff. Dr. J. W. Storer, a wonderful friend for many years, described the work of president of the Convention as well as anyone.

"Primarily the president is elected to preside over the sessions of the Southern Baptist Convention. He is to do this with fairness to every messenger—even to the cliques that buzz around him, on platform, in lobby, and elsewhere. He is to preside with dignity and not forget that he is one of the brethren—not sacrosanct nor beyond making mistakes.

"He should be firm but not stern. If possible his knowledge of parliamentary law and the Southern Baptist Convention constitution and bylaws should be as nearly complete as he can make it.

"Between sessions he must remember that he is *not* the voice of either the Convention, the churches, or of any Baptist other than himself. Others may *assume* he is, but he must never give any ground for such assumption.

"He is not the Southern Baptist Convention politician sounding forth on any political platform or parading his personal opinions—no matter how great the desire to do so. . . .

"It seems to me the travelogue is worked overtime. How can any man, even a president of the Southern Baptist Convention, flit from continent to continent, presume to have time or perspicacity enough to formulate an accurate estimation of either the needs or problems of our mission fields? Not to mention the encroachment on the too worn hospitality of the missionaries.

"I believe our presidents should rather confine their journeys to the state conventions and not spread themselves too thin. There they should address themselves to what the Book says and not on what the newspapers report. Give the conventions a rallying call to the teachings once for all delivered to the saints. Here be it remembered he cannot 'make' all the conventions—their scheduled meetings and his time will not permit it.

"Bearing in mind that most of our presidents are pastors, they have a responsibility to their individual churches which cannot be waived. No man called of God to be the pastor of a church dare neglect that church in order to serve as president of the Southern Baptist Convention. Greater is the pastorate than the presidency—greater in honor, greater in service, and I believe greater in the sight of God.

"He can, based on his experience and observation as a denominational servant, give his advice when it is sought, and with perfect propriety. But never from a plank one inch from the floor on which others stand. And, if it is not taken, let that be the end of the matter—no controversy, please, above all, through the denominational press."

Porter Routh

William B. Johnson
1845-1849

George Washington, first president of the United States, went to Georgetown, South Carolina, in 1791 for a reception; and one of the admirers to shake his hand was a nine-year-old lad—William Bullein Johnson, who some fifity years later, in 1845, was to become the first president of the Southern Baptist Convention.

Dr. Johnson remembered with pleasure his meeting with George Washington, but it was a meeting with Luther Rice at the Savannah River Association in 1813 that was to have greater meaning in his life. When Luther Rice told of the experience he had shared with Adoniram Judson in going to India, W. B. Johnson caught a world vision he was never to lose.

The Savannah River Missionary Society, one of the first in the South, was organized immediately after Rice's visit, and Johnson became the first president. He suggested that the meeting place for representatives of other mission societies be Philadelphia; and when the Triennial Convention was organized in 1814, Dr. Johnson not only served on the committee to draft the constitution, but was also named as the

9

corresponding secretary of its Foreign Mission Board.

As a young man, W. B. Johnson had studied law and had attended Brown University. This training was of real value as he not only assisted in preparing the constitution for the Triennial Convention, but also served on the committee preparing the constitution when the South Carolina Convention was organized in 1821 and when the Southern Baptist Convention was organized in Augusta, Georgia, in 1845.

As president of the Triennial Convention from 1841 to 1845, Dr. Johnson did much to try to iron out the differences between the North and the South, but finally he came to the conclusion that greater good could be accomplished through two conventions. He told the Savannah River Association shortly after the Augusta Convention: "Our objects then are the extension of the Messiah's kingdom, and the glory of our God. Not disunion with any of his people; not the upholding of any form of human policy, or civil rights; but God's glory, and Messiah's increasing reign."

Dr. Johnson's crowning work was the part he played in the organization of the Southern Baptist Theological Seminary, and he had the pleasure of being present in Greenville for the opening session in 1859 to offer the dedicatory prayer.

William Bullein Johnson died in Greenville, South Carolina, on October 2, 1862. He had dedicated his life to the uniting of Southern Baptists for the projection of the great missionary fire that burned in his heart. He had given a son as one of the first of Southern Baptists' missionaries to China.

In her excellent biography of William Bullein Johnson, *Giant in the Land*, Hortense Caroline Woodson tells of Dr. Johnson's conversation with his granddaughter on the last day of his life.

"How grateful you must be, Grandfather, for doing so much good!" Ella remarked.

Grandfather murmured very softly, "Not unto me, not unto me—but to Thy Name, O God, be all the glory!"

R. B. C. Howell
1851-1857

A tall, thin youth in homespun clothes, just barely out of his teens, was baptized into the fellowship of the Nanchanty Baptist Church, about fourteen miles from Raleigh, North Carolina, on February 6, 1821.

The day was crisp, and the water was cold; but there was a warm glow in the heart of Robert Boyte Crawford Howell which was to remain until his death, nearly fifty years later. And on the very next Sunday, the young man was to take as his text Matthew 11:2-6 and preach on the infinite grace manifested in the gospel of Christ. By the time he left for Columbian College the next fall, he had won two hundred others to Jesus as Savior.

In college, R. B. C. Howell was torn between God's call to the ministry and preparation for law. It was not until he had twice been called by the Cumberland Street Baptist Church at Norfolk, Virginia, that he would allow himself to be ordained on January 7, 1827.

In 1835, R. B. C. Howell was called as pastor of the struggling First Baptist Church in Nashville, Tennessee. The church had almost lost its life in 1830 when all but five members followed Alexander Campbell to establish another church. Dr. Howell remained in Nashville until 1849. He baptized 392 persons, led in building a house of worship, and saw twenty-three young men go out to preach. During this same period, Dr. Howell started *The Baptist,* later joined with *The Reflector* to become the official Baptist paper of Tennessee.

When the Southern Baptist Convention was organized in 1845, R. B. C. Howell was named on the committee to obtain the charter from the state of Georgia. He gave the Convention his full support and was a logical person to succeed Dr. William B. Johnson as president when the Convention met in Nashville in 1851. Dr. Howell was then serving as pastor of the Second Baptist Church, Richmond, Virginia.

William B. Johnson gave organizational direction as the first president. R. B. C. Howell gave doctrinal solidarity. He was a great teacher and had much to do with the organization of the Southern Baptist Theological Seminary. He was a fluent writer, and his opinions were respected by ministers in all sections of the United States.

In 1857, while serving his third term as president of the Southern Baptist Convention, Dr. Howell returned to the First Baptist Church, Nashville, as pastor. He was elected for a fourth term when the Convention met in Richmond in 1859; but as he was engaged in a fierce theological dispute at that time, he immediately resigned rather than have his own dispute endanger the Convention.

R. B. C. Howell died in Nashville on April 5, 1868.

Richard Fuller
1859-1861

First in his class at Harvard at the age of sixteen! An outstanding South Carolina attorney at the age of twenty-four! A prominent layman in the Episcopal Church at the age of twenty-four! A Baptist preacher at the age of twenty-eight! The third president of the Southern Baptist Convention at the age of fifty-five!

If Richard Fuller were living today instead of in the last century, his decisions would be the subject for many newspaper feature stories. He was born at Beaufort, South Carolina, April 22, 1804. Young Richard entered Harvard with literary ambitions; but in his senior year, he had a hemorrhage of the lungs and had to withdraw. He returned to Beaufort and turned his attention to the law. At the age of twenty-eight, he was making more than $6,000 a year, a fabulous sum in that time. He was being mentioned for high political office in South Carolina.

In 1831 Richard Fuller had united with the Episcopal Church. However, in the same year, he heard a great Baptist evangelist, Daniel Baker; and he realized that his days as a lawyer were ended. He was baptized into the fellowship of the Baptist church in Beaufort. The next year he was called as pastor at Beaufort and "resolved never to insult the Master with indolent preparation or superficial and ineffectual performance." It is reported that he baptized one hundred converts on the day he was ordained in 1832.

In 1847 Richard Fuller was called as pastor in Baltimore, where he remained until his death. He is listed as the preacher of the first Convention sermon, and his message on "The Cross," with the text taken from John 12:32, was preached with such power that he was asked to preach at some time during each Convention until 1862. As he passed away on October 20, 1876, he murmured again and again, "Who'll preach Jesus?"

P. H. Mell
1863-1871, 1880-1887

Penfield Baptist Church in Georgia sent a young minister, thirty-year-old Patrick Hues Mell, to the organizational meeting of the Southern Baptist Convention at Augusta, Georgia, in 1845. In 1863, during the dark days of the War Between the States, Dr. Mell was elected president of the Convention. He served for seventeen years, the longest period served by any man in the organization's history.

Patrick Hues Mell was born May 19, 1814, in Walthourville, Georgia. He studied in the academies in Liberty County in his boyhood, and then attended Amherst College in Massachusetts for two years. After teaching school in south Georgia for several years, he became professor of ancient languages at Mercer University in 1842. His relationship with Mercer was dissolved in 1855 when he was elected to the faculty at Georgia University. He rose to the position of chancellor before his death at Athens, Georgia, in 1888.

The same year Patrick Hues Mell was elected to the faculty of Mercer University, he was also ordained as a preacher by the Penfield Baptist Church. For twenty-three years he was

15

pastor of the Bairdstown church and for twenty-eight years he served as pastor of the Antioch church in Oglethorpe County. He served both of these country churches in addition to his duties with Mercer and the University of Georgia.

From 1872 until 1880 Dr. Mell was not able to attend the sessions of the Convention because of illness, but he was elected president again in 1880. He served until his death in 1888.

"President Mell," as he was aptly called, also presided for twenty-nine years over the Georgia district association and for twenty-five years over the Georgia Baptist Convention. A prolific writer, Dr. Mell wrote *Manual of Parliamentary Practice* which was used as the rules of order for the Convention for a number of years. His book *Corrective Church Discipline* set the stage for a dispute on church government that spread over the entire Southland.

An account in a Texas newspaper of the session of the Southern Baptist Convention in Waco in 1883 contains the following reference to him: "The Southern Baptists can never cease to admire the genius of Dr. Mell as a presiding officer. He rules with the inflexible rigor of a tyrant, and yet with a spirit so genial and sympathetic that no reasonable man can ever be embarrassed by his presence."

James P. Boyce
1872-1879, 1888

About 1683 two groups of settlers arrived in South Carolina, near Charles Town. One group came from the west of England. The second group came from Kittery, in the state of Maine. Love of truth and persecution for belief was a common experience, and it was not long before they were joined in what was to become the First Baptist Church of Charleston, South Carolina.

This church was to produce many outstanding Baptist characters in the years ahead. One of the most illustrious of her sons was James Pettigru Boyce, the fifth president of the Southern Baptist Convention. He was born in Charleston on January 11, 1827. His father was one of the financial leaders of the old South. Among the Sunday School teachers of young Boyce were Charles H. Lanneau, one of the great laymen of his day, and Henry Allen Tupper, who later became secretary of the Southern Baptist Foreign Mission Board.

While Young Boyce was a student in Brown University, from which he was graduated in 1847, he accepted Christ and was baptized by the Reverend Richard Fuller in 1846. After

17

completing his work at Brown, he felt the call to enter the ministry, and entered the Princeton Theological Seminary. In 1851 he was ordained and called as pastor of the Baptist church at Columbia, South Carolina.

While teaching at Furman, James P. Boyce saw the need for a theological seminary for the Southern Baptist Convention. He poured his life and his wealth into the founding of the Southern Baptist Theological Seminary. He was the first chairman of the faculty and the first general agent. In the dark days following the Civil War, he was offered $10,000 a year, a fabulous salary for that time, to serve as president of a railroad. Even though the seminary could not pay his salary at the time, he replied, "Thank the gentlemen for me; but tell them I must decline, as I have decided to devote my life, if need be, to building the Southern Baptist Theological Seminary."

Writing of Dr. Boyce as president of the Southern Baptist Convention, Dr. John A. Broadus penned: "To preside well over a big Baptist convention is no ordinary task; the Speaker in the national House of Representatives . . . has scarcely greater difficulties to overcome. Every Baptist of them all feels himself perfectly free, and wishes to be personally uncontrolled, and yet all desire that the president shall maintain perfect order." Dr. Boyce met those qualifications.

Dr. Boyce went to France in 1888 for his health and died at Pau, in the south of France, on December 28, 1888.

Jonathan Haralson
1889-1898

When the thirty-fourth session of the Southern Baptist Convention was called to order on May 10, 1889, in the First Baptist Church, Memphis, Tennessee, the president's chair was empty. President James P. Boyce had died during the year, and there was some confusion when Lewis Bell Ely of Carrollton, Missouri, took the gavel and called for the organization of the Convention.

In those early days the election of officers was one of the first items of business. When the nominations were opened, Dr. M. B. Wharton of Montgomery, Alabama, a man of wide experience and acquaintance in the South, nominated Judge Jonathan Haralson, a layman he had come to know and love in Alabama. When the votes were counted, Judge Haralson, who had been elected as a vice-president in 1887, was the new president, the first layman to hold that office in the history of the Convention.

Jonathan Haralson was born in Lowndes County, Alabama, October 18, 1830. He attended the University of Alabama while Dr. Basil Manly was serving as president and then went on to Louisiana, where he completed his work in a law school in New Orleans in 1852. He settled in Selma in 1853, just at the time Baptist work was being firmly established there. His first pastor was Reverend A. G. McCraw, a man with a vision reaching to the ends of the earth. Other pastors who served during the period Jonathan Haralson lived at Selma were the eloquent J. B. Hawthorne and the tireless J. M. Frost, who later was to take the lead in the organization of the present Sunday School Board.

Judge Haralson went to Europe on several legal cases, served with distinction in the lower courts of Alabama, and climaxed his legal service as an associate justice of the Supreme Court of Alabama from 1892 until 1910.

He applied the same industry to the activities of his church and denomination that he did to his legal career. In 1874 he was elected as president of the Alabama state convention, and he served with distinction until 1891 when he was elected as president of the Southern Baptist Convention, a position he held for ten years.

After Judge Haralson's death at Montgomery, Alabama, on July 11, 1912, Dr. J. M. Frost wrote: "I have seen mighty men as presiding officers, but to my thinking and yet without disparagement to others, I never saw his superior in wielding the gavel and directing the forces of a great assembly. He was equally great whether the Convention was in a mighty storm, as sometimes happened in those days, or was under the influence of a great surging wave of spiritual influence."

W. J. Northen
1899-1901

William Jonathan Northen, who started the custom of shorter terms for presidents of the Southern Baptist Convention, was the product of a Christian home and a Christian school.

His father, Peter Northen, had long been a leading layman in the Georgia Baptist Convention; and young William followed in the steps of his father. One of eleven children, he was born in Jones County, Georgia, on July 9, 1835. When W. J. was five years old, his father moved to Penfield where he took charge of Steward's Hall at Mercer University. Thus the young man grew up in the shadow of the great Georgia Baptist college and received his degree from that school in 1853.

For nearly twenty years after graduation, with the exception of a period during the Civil War when he served as a private in a company raised by his father, W. J. Northen served as principal of Mount Zion Academy in Hancock County. He gained such a reputation in the field of agriculture that he was elected president of the State Agricultural Society in 1886. For the next four years he mixed farming and politics, and he was elected governor in 1890.

From 1896 to 1908 William Northen was president of the Georgia Baptist Convention, and from 1898 through 1901 he was president of the Southern Baptist Convention. He was a trustee of Mercer University from 1869 until his death on March 25, 1913. From the time he moved to Penfield until his death, it was said that he seldom missed a commencement exercise at Mercer.

After his death, the *Baptist Standard* of Texas carried this observation: "Governor Northen was a devout, self-sacrificing Christian. This shone in his church, his community, his state; everywhere he lent his novel, genial presence."

James P. Eagle
1902-1904

James Philip Eagle, the eighth president of the Southern Baptist Convention, had the unique distinction of winning fame as a soldier, a farmer, a legislator, a preacher, a governor, and a denominational leader.

He was born in Maury County, Tennessee, on August 10, 1837; but at an early age he moved with his parents to Lonoke, Arkansas. As he grew up on a farm, his formal education was limited; but he was diligent in developing his native abilities. One of his outstanding characteristics was the ability to win the confidence of people. He enlisted in 1861 as a private in the Confederate Army and rapidly climbed to the rank of lieutenant colonel.

It was not until his return to his farm home after the war that J. P. Eagle became a Christian. He was baptized by Elder Moses Green at the New Hope Church in 1857, and he was ordained as a minister two years later. Two other interests claimed the attention of the young farmer and minister at the time. His friends sent him to the state legislature in 1873, where he served with distinction until his election as governor in 1889. And he met Mary Kavanaugh Oldham of Kentucky, who, after a courtship lasting fourteen years, became Mrs. Eagle.

J. P. Eagle had been elected as president of the Arkansas Baptist Convention in 1880, and Mrs. Eagle became an active leader in the work of the Woman's Missionary Union after their marriage in 1882.

During all the period he was in public life, he continued to expand his farm holdings. He served a number of rural churches as pastor but would never accept a cent as salary.

Before his election as president of the Southern Baptist Convention in 1902, Governor Eagle had served for several years as vice-president. Always he was a worker for peace and unity in denominational affairs.

Mr. Eagle was a member of the first committee to consider establishing Ouachita College, and he remained a friend to the school until his death on December 20, 1904. Although he was in feeble health, he attended the meeting of the state convention just a few weeks before his death and made a plea for increased support for Ouachita. He left the school $13,160 in his will.

Although he died at the comparatively early age of sixty-seven, he had filled those years with service to his God and to his fellowman.

E. W. Stephens
1905-1907

Edwin William Stephens, the ninth president of the Southern Baptist Convention, served as president of thirty-five different boards, commissions, conventions, and associations during his life.

He was moderator of his association, moderator of the Missouri Baptist Association, vice-president of the Northern Baptist Convention, president of the Southern Baptist Convention, president of the short-lived Baptist General Convention of America, and American treasurer of the Baptist World Alliance.

In secular life, E. W. was editor and publisher of the *Columbia Herald* for thirty-five years, president of the E. W. Stephens Publishing Company, of the National Editorial Association, and of the YMCA of Missouri.

Edwin Stephens was born in Columbia, Missouri, January 21, 1849. His father, James L. Stephens, had come to Missouri from Kentucky in 1919 and had soon establishing a thriving business. His contributions made possible the early work of Stephens College.

James L. Stephens had played a big part in the location of the University of Missouri at Columbia. E. W. inherited his father's interest in the University of Missouri and was also very much interested in William Jewell College. He had much to do with the founding of the famous school of journalism at the University of Missouri.

Since President Eagle had died during the year, the Southern Baptist Convention had no president when its session opened in Kansas City in 1905. When W. E. Hatcher of Virginia nominated E. W. Stephens for president, he said, "In the field of business and also in the field of Christian fellowship, he has shown himself to be a man of great power." Dr. T. T. Eaton of Kentucky, who had also been nominated, asked that his name be withdrawn and made the motion that the secretary be asked to cast a unanimous vote for Mr. Stephens.

After his election as president of the Southern Baptist Convention, Mr. Stephens made a world tour. He represented Southern Baptists at the meeting of the Baptist World Alliance, and his speech before twelve thousand people in the great Albert Hall in London demonstrated his grasp of Baptist opportunities in the world.

President Stephens made an excellent presiding officer, and as one writer phrased it, "He knew just when to yield the rigid letter of parliamentary law in the interest of good humor that occasionally seeks demonstrations in a great religious body." It is interesting to note that the Convention, meeting in 1905, voted to ask the president to deliver a stated address at the meeting in 1906. His address at Chattanooga stands as one of the classics among Convention addresses. It was distributed widely by the Sunday School Board in tract form at that time, and it concluded: "It will not be until the world shall have reached the state of political freedom set forth in the Declaration of Independence, that all men are born free and equal, and until the Bible is read, free of all prejudice or dictation, ecclesiastical, political, or social, that Baptists will be recognized and valued, and will value themselves for what they really are."

Although Mr. Stephens had a vision of the world opportunities which Baptists faced, he never lost interest in the work of his own church, the First Baptist Church of Columbia, Missouri. In addition to other activities, he taught a Sunday School class there for thirty-one years.

A lifelong resident of Columbia, Mr. Stephens died there on May 22, 1931, at the age of eighty-three.

Joshua Levering
1908-1910

One of the great Baptist laymen of the past century was Eugene Levering, Sr., of Baltimore, Maryland. With his brother, he built one of the largest coffee importing and shipping concerns in the United States.

Eugene Levering, Sr., not only developed a great business, but he also developed a Christian home. Among his twelve children were twins, Eugene, Jr., and Joshua, born on September 12, 1845. Richard Fuller, one of the leading Baptist ministers of his day, was a frequent visitor in the home and guided the family in making Christ the center of all life.

An example of their Christian attitude in all areas of life is demonstrated in one incident in the life of the father. Much of the firm's business was in the South. When the War Between the States broke out in 1861, the business was forced to settle more than $100,000 in debts for half of the value. When good business returned after the war, the firm redeemed all debts in full, although there was no legal obligation.

The sons continued to build the business, and both of them continued their interest in Christian activities.

One of the early leaders in the Prohibition movement in the United States, Joshua Levering was the Prohibition candidate for President of the United States in 1896. For many years he was the president of the board of trustees of the Southern Baptist Theological Seminary in Louisville. His gifts made possible the building of the Levering Gymnasium on the seminary campus. He also served as a member of the Foreign Mission Board; and it is reported that the Bagbys, first Southern Baptist missionaries to Brazil, went out on a Levering ship.

In 1908 Joshua Levering became president of the Southern Baptist Convention and served through 1910.

He died in Baltimore on October 5, 1935, at the age of ninety-one.

Edwin C. Dargan
1911-1913

After the meeting of the Southern Baptist Convention in Jacksonville, Florida, in 1911, Dr. George W. Truett wrote in the Texas *Baptist Standard*: "Dr. E. C. Dargan, so long a professor of Southern, but now pastor of the First Church, Macon, Georgia, is making a superb president. He allowed not a minute to be lost. And his honored predecessor, Brother Joshua Levering of Baltimore, was constantly on hand to give his noblest co-operation."

The election of Dr. Dargan had come as a real surprise. Everyone had thought that Joshua Levering of Maryland would be reelected. But Henry Seay, a quiet businessman from Virginia, thought that it was time for a minister to serve as president. When the nominations were opened, Mr. Seay looked about him for Dr. S. C. Mitchell of South Carolina but did not see him. He noticed Dr. Dargan sitting a few seats in front of him and nominated him.

Much to the surprise of all—and especially to the surprise of Dr. Dargan—the majority, without discredit to Mr. Levering, joined the Virginia layman in thinking that it was time for a change.

Edwin Charles Dargan was the product of a distinguished Baptist family, but he won positions of responsibility on his own merit. He was born in Darlington County, South Carolina, November 17, 1852. At twenty-one he was a graduate of Furman University, Greenville, South Carolina; at twenty-five he was a graduate of the Southern Baptist Theological Seminary, then located at Greenville. Honorary degrees were later conferred upon him by Baylor University and also by Washington and Lee University.

After serving several small churches in Virginia, Dr. Dargan felt the urge to "go West" and accepted the pastorate of the Baptist church in Dixon, California. But after two years he returned to South Carolina to become pastor of the Citadel Square Church in Charleston.

In 1892 Dr. Dargan was elected professor in the Southern Seminary. He became an authority in the field of ecclesiology and preaching and wrote two books on the history of preaching. He was also a great lover of music and an authority on hymnology.

But Dr. Dargan did not lose his love for preaching in his study of preaching. In 1907 he accepted a call to the pastorate of the First Church, Macon, one of the most effective pulpits of that day.

He remained in Macon until 1917 when he responded to the call of the Sunday School Board to join with Dr. Hight C Moore in editing the publications of the Board. He remained as editor of Sunday School lesson helps until he retired in 1927. His working library he bequeathed to the Sunday School Board as a reference library for editors and other employees, and it was named in his honor. Then in 1951 the collections of the Historical Commission were merged with the Dargan Memorial Library, and the name was changed in 1953 to Dargan-Carver Library. It has become the major historical resource for Southern Baptists as well as a valuable, specialized library for Board personnel.

Dr. Dargan died at the home of a son in Chicago on October 26, 1930. As one editor expressed it, "He was a giant in intellect and spirit, but as simple and humble in manner as a little child."

Lansing Burrows
1914-1916

John Lansing Burrows was the twelfth president of the Southern Baptist Convention, but he will be remembered best in Southern Baptist history for his pioneering work in the collection of data from Southern Baptist churches and for his thirty-two years' service as the senior secretary of the Convention.

At the meeting of the Southern Baptist Convention at Columbus, Mississippi, in 1881, J. Lansing Burrows was nominated by James P. Boyce as the assistant secretary. In 1882 he was elected as secretary and brought in his first statistical report. A special committee appointed to study it brought in this report:

"We regard the Report as perhaps the most valuable contribution which has been made to the history of Southern Baptists in many years . . . We recommend that the thanks of this body be returned to brother Lansing Burrows, for the laborious task which he has so cheerfully and faithfully performed, and that he be requested to continue in the good work. . . ."

Lansing Burrows did continue in the good work and recorded in large ledger books, now in Nashville, in his own handwriting, the record of each church in the entire Convention.

This interest in Southern Baptist life was a natural thing for young Lansing. His father, John Burrows, a distinguished Baptist minister, had attended the organizational meeting of the Southern Baptist Convention in 1845. Mr. Burrows was then pastor in Philadelphia, where young Lansing had been born in April 1843.

While his father was pastor in Richmond, Virginia, young Lansing entered Richmond College, but he later transferred to Wake Forest College. As his schooling was interrupted by service in the Confederate Army, he did not receive his diploma until after the war. Feeling that the Lord had called him to preach, he was ordained at Stanford, Kentucky, in 1867.

After receiving his degree from Princeton in 1871, Lansing Burrows served churches in New Jersey until he returned to Lexington, Kentucky, in 1879. He later served as pastor at Augusta, Georgia; Nashville, Tennessee; and Americus, Georgia. He was living at Americus at the time of his death on October 17, 1917.

After Dr. Lansing Burrows had served his first year as president of the Convention, the editor of the *Alabama Baptist* wrote: "He was standing like a bull at bay with hair pointed outward, ready to throw over the fence all who failed to get into the field in any other way than through the parliamentary gate. On Sunday, he was transformed into an angel of sweetness."

J. B. Gambrell
1917-1920

"More people, a hundred to one, will join in a bear hunt than will turn out to kill a mouse."

"A desire to get up in the ministry has kept many a man down in the ministry."

"A degree is like a promissory note. The value of it depends on what is back of it."

"I could never admire the dog with a noble voice that gave its nights to barking at crickets."

"Mud will rub off much easier when it is dry."

"It is no time, in a charge, to stop to sew on buttons."

These are but a few of the quotations picked at random from the many sage observations of J. B. Gambrell. For "Uncle Gideon," as he was affectionately known by thousands of Southern Baptist ministers, had a pithy way of putting things that would clear the atmosphere and make right decisions easy. "As Dr. Gambrell used to say" is still a familiar phrase used by many Southern Baptist preachers.

James Bruton Gambrell was born in Anderson County, South Carolina, August 21, 1841. The family soon moved to

Mississippi, and it is reported that the father missed only two services in twenty-five years as a faithful member of the old Pleasant Ridge Baptist Church in Mississippi.

During the War Between the States, young Gambrell enlisted in a company commanded by his teacher, Captain R. M. Leavell; and he became a daring scout in the Confederate Army.

In 1866 he was licensed to preach by the Pleasant Ridge Church, and the next year the Cherry Creek Church ordained him. While attending the University of Mississippi, he served as pastor at Oxford.

During his five years at Oxford, J. B. Gambrell gained such a wide reputation as a writer that he was elected editor of the Mississippi *Baptist Record.* Soon the attention of the entire South was focused on his editorials.

A great believer in education, Dr. Gambrell served as president of Mercer University in Georgia for a short time. However, because he enjoyed closer contact with the masses of Baptists than was possible on a college campus, when the call came to serve as mission secretary in Texas, he accepted. Texas Baptists were facing difficult days in 1896 when Dr. Gambrell unpacked, but his ready wit and his Christian courage set the stage for progress. He was aided greatly by his gifted wife, who was elected secretary of the women's missionary work. He later served as editor of the *Baptist Standard* and as professor in Southwestern Baptist Seminary.

J. B. Gambrell was seventy-six when elected president of the Southern Baptist Convention, but he was well preserved and a man of great vigor. While he was president of the Convention, women were first admitted as messengers, the Relief and Annuity Board was created, the Seventy-five Million Campaign was launched, and Baptists rejected the bid of the Inter-Church movement. Southern Baptists have never wavered from the stand Dr. Gambrell took at a tense moment in the Southern Baptist Convention when he declared, "Southern Baptists do not ride a horse without a bridle."

Just a month before his death, J. B. Gambrell, flat on his back with heart disease, wrote a little article, "Incidents and Meditation," which was published in several Southern Baptist papers. A month after his death, a letter came from a lonely missionary in China saying, "Your message helped with its clear, confident note of faith in God, and his willingness to help. I am sure He will see me through this decision. You have been a tower of strength to me all my life"

The great commoner among Southern Baptists died in Dallas, Texas on June 10, 1921.

E. Y. Mullins
1921-1923

On January 5, 1860, a young pastor of a country Baptist church in Franklin County, Mississippi, knelt by the crib of his firstborn son and prayed earnestly that someday God might call the boy to be a minister of the gospel.

The child was given the name Edgar Young Mullins. He not only became a minister, but lived to serve as president of the Southern Baptist Theological Seminary, of the Southern Baptist Convention, and of the Baptist World Alliance.

In 1868 the Mullins family moved to Corsicana, Texas. Because there were eleven children in the family, young Edgar sought and found employment as a messenger boy and later as a telegrapher to help meet expenses. He even helped pay for his older sisters to attend Baylor.

Young Mullins planned to study law—not to preach; at the time of his graduation from Texas A. and M. he had not even accepted Christ as his Savior. He was working in Dallas as an expert telegrapher for the Associated Press when, on October 30, 1880, he went with a friend to hear Major W. E. Penn, the evangelist. God touched his heart, and that night he accepted

Jesus as Savior and Lord. He was baptized by his happy father the next week.

When Edgar Young Mullins accepted Christ, he surrendered all of life. He entered the seminary at Louisville in 1881 and received his degree for the full course in 1885. A few weeks after graduation, on June 6, he was ordained by the First Baptist Church at Harrodsburg, Kentucky, to which he had been called as pastor. A year later he married Isla May Hawley.

The young couple had a desire to go to Brazil as missionaries, but the financial condition of the Foreign Mission Board closed that door. Later, in 1896, Dr. Mullins did serve for a brief period as associate secretary of the Foreign Mission Board.

On June 29, 1899, Dr. Mullins was called to lead the Southern Baptist Theological Seminary as president during a period of crisis in the history of the school. He accepted the responsibility and served with great distinction until his death on November 23, 1928. He led in the building of the new seminary campus; and great scholar that he was, he made a tremendous contribution to Southern Baptist life, particularly through his books: *The Axioms of Religion, Baptist Beliefs,* and *The Christian Religion in Its Doctrinal Expression.*

It is interesting to note that Dr. Mullins always kept his Bible by his bed. It was the first thing he touched in the morning and the last word he read each night.

Dr. W. O. Carver wrote in tribute to Dr. Mullins at the time of his death: "Dr. Mullins stands in the minds of those who knew him best as an intelligent, determined, conquering instrument of the redemptive will of God. He led by following Jesus Christ."

George W. McDaniel
1924-1926

Have you ever heard of a minister who refused to accept the pastorate of a large wealthy church until some of the members changed their business?

This is exactly what happened when George White McDaniel was called as pastor of the First Baptist Church of Richmond, Virginia. The young minister, only thirty years of age at the time, refused to accept the call because he found "two members engaged in a business which I could not countenance." The two members agreed to change their business, and young McDaniel accepted the call.

This illustration from the life of George White McDaniel, fifteenth president of the Southern Baptist Convention, is an index to the character and convictions which characterized this Southern Baptist leader.

George White McDaniel was born in Grimes County, Texas, on November 30, 1875. Both parents died when young George was sixteen. The year after their deaths he was converted in a Methodist revival. He started to join the Methodist church, but his sister asked him to wait until he had read his

New Testament more. He then decided to join a Baptist church and was baptized in the First Baptist Church at Navasto.

After his conversion, George decided to attend Baylor University. While a student there he lived in the home of Dr. B. H. Carroll. In his senior year, he married one of his professors, Martha Douglass Scarborough. After seminary training at the Southern Seminary at Louisville, he was called to the church at Temple, Texas. Later he was called to the Gaston Avenue Church, Dallas, and finally to the First Church, Richmond, where he served as pastor for nearly twenty-three years before his untimely death on August 20, 1927.

Like Dr. Gambrell, Dr. McDaniel was a great lover of dogs, and like Dr. Gambrell he was a strong fighter for Baptist fundamentals. When Southern Baptists were torn on some issue, they could nearly always find common ground in the positive affirmations made by George McDaniel.

In the presidential address at St. Louis in 1927, Dr. McDaniel said: "We have but one authoritative guide in faith—the New Testament—to which the hearts of our people beat true. We are more nearly one in doctrine than any other religious group of similar size. We might wisely emphasize our agreements. Blessed be God that individual freedom has voiced common agreement once and again through the Southern Baptist Convention. Therefore, leaving the principles of the doctrines of Christ, on which we have remarkable unanimity, let us go on with the practical tasks of the Convention, not reviving discussion upon questions already settled as far as they may be settled among a free people."

Dr. George W. Truett went from Dallas to preach the funeral service of Dr. McDaniel. Among other things he said, "As a presiding officer, he will go down in history with men like Boyce and Mell and Judge Haralson."

George W. Truett
1927-1929

Shortly before the death of Dr. George W. Truett on July 8, 1944, a friend visited the famous preacher. Aware of Dr. Truett's inability to sleep because of his intense suffering, the friend asked if the nights did not seem long.

"No!" Dr. Truett replied firmly. "I start counting the good things God has done for me, and the kindnesses of many friends, and the nights are not long enough."

At the time of Dr. Truett's death the secret of his preaching was said to be this: Like many other preachers, Dr. Truett spent many hours preparing his sermon—but he spent many more hours preparing himself in prayer.

These two illustrations reflect something of the character of the man who has been called the greatest preacher produced by Southern Baptists.

George Washington Truett was born in a humble home on May 6, 1867, in Clay County, North Carolina. At the age of nineteen, he was converted in a rural revival while teaching at the Crooked Creek School. A short time after his conversion, the family moved to Texas.

Ordained as a minister by the Whitewright Baptist Church in 1890, he soon won a wide reputation as a preacher. Shortly thereafter Texas Baptists asked him to lead in a campaign to free Baylor from debt. When the campaign was completed in 1893, Mr. Truett entered Baylor as a freshman. He served as pastor in Waco while he was in school. In 1894 he married Josephine Jenkins.

When George W. Truett graduated from Baylor in 1897, he was called to the pastorate of the First Baptist Church in Dallas, where he remained until his death.

Dr. Truett was offered the presidency of Baylor University, and in later years he was offered many of the great pastorates of the United States. He had much to do with the starting of Baylor Hospital, the Relief and Annuity Board, and the Southwestern Seminary. Three times he was elected president of the Southern Baptist Convention. He also presided over three sessions of the Baptist World Alliance. His missionary journeys around the world meant much to the cause of Christ. His address at Washington in 1920, before a crowd of twenty thousand, is considered one of the finest statements ever made on the subject of religious liberty.

W. J. McGlothlin
1930-1932

At the turn of the last century, Southern Baptists were seriously divided over the writings of William H. Whitsitt, president of the Southern Baptist Theological Seminary and professor of church history in the school.

When Dr. Whitsitt resigned in 1899, attention was focused on the chair of church history at the school. Who would be the new professor of church history?

Dr. E. Y. Mullins, the newly elected president, thought at first that he would take the trouble spot; but he turned to theology, and the important position was given to William Joseph McGlothlin. Under the guidance of John R. Sampey, the young man had already shown himself to be a Hebrew scholar; and he later grew to be a real authority in the field of church history.

William Joseph McGlothlin was born near Gallatin, Tennessee, on November 29, 1867. He attended the rural schools of his community and later completed his college work at Bethel College in Kentucky. He taught in the public schools to finance his way through college.

Ordained as a minister in 1891, he entered the Southern Baptist Theological Seminary the same year. After graduation in 1894, he was selected by Dr. Sampey as his assistant. He taught in the area of Old Testament and Hebrew until he was elected as professor of church history. In order to prepare himself better, he went to Germany to study and received his Ph.D. from the University of Berlin in 1901.

In 1914 Dr. McGlothlin was elected president of Furman University in South Carolina. He remained there until his untimely death on May 28, 1933, following an automobile accident on the way to the meeting of the Southern Baptist Convention in Washington. He had been elected president of the Convention in 1930 and had served for three years.

Among his books which won recognition are: *A Guide to the Study of Church History,* published in 1908; *Infant Baptism in History,* published in 1915; and *The Course of Christian History,* 1917.

When Dr. McGlothlin died, Z. T. Cody, editor of the South Carolina *Baptist Courier,* wrote: "As president of the Convention, he rendered a notable service, for he brought to the great office not only a perfect knowledge of parliamentary law, but also an understanding of the complicated official life of Southern Baptists and an unwearied purpose to preserve our Baptist polity when the pressure of denominational problems was threatening its integrity."

Fred F. Brown
1933

When the story of Southern Baptists' recovery from the financial disaster which almost overcame many of the denominational agencies in the early 1930s is finally written, the name of Frederick Fernando Brown will stand high on the list of those who saw victory through the clouds.

Jackson County, almost lost in the mountains of North Carolina, is not known for its rich farmlands, but it will long be remembered as the birthplace of Fred Brown. On November 27, 1882, at the home of Mr. and Mrs. Horace Alonzo Brown, the future leader of Southern Baptists first saw the light of day. He left the small hamlet of Glenville in his young manhood, but he was never able to get away from the rugged honesty and the firm convictions which are a part of the mountain people of North Carolina.

After attending Mars Hill College in North Carolina, Fred Brown went on to Wake Forest College, where he received his master's degree in 1909. He received his Th.M. degree at Southern Baptist Seminary in 1912, and the following year he completed the work for his doctorate. He was ordained in 1913.

After pastorates at Harrodsburg and Frankfort in Kentucky, Fred Brown was called to Sherman, Texas, where he stayed until 1921 when he was called to the First Baptist Church, Knoxville, Tennessee. He remained there as pastor until his retirement from the active pastorate in 1946.

After the stock market crash in October, 1929, many Southern Baptist institutions found their operations difficult. Their debts amounted to nearly $6,000,000. The financial picture was gloomy when the newly organized Promotion Committee met in Birmingham, Alabama, on July 7, 1931.

Members of the Promotion Committee looked to Dr. Brown to lead Southern Baptists in a campaign to pay their debts, to magnify the every-member canvass, and to enlist one million tithers. Dr. Brown did not feel that he could leave his pastorate; but the First Church, Knoxville, recognizing the need, unselfishly released their pastor until the next session of the Convention and continued to pay his salary. Dr. Brown threw himself, without reserve, into the campaign. It was little wonder that he was elected president of the Convention in St. Petersburg in 1932. During the next year, he literally wore himself out traveling over the territory of the Southern Baptist Convention.

Dr. Brown is the only man elected president of the Southern Baptist Convention who never presided over a session; for the year he was elected was the first year the president was elected at the end of the session. The next year he was ill at the time of the Convention and was not reelected.

Dr. Brown continued to live in Knoxville until his death on August 9, 1960.

M. E. Dodd
1934-1935

"In this, the Baptist missionary hour of all the centuries, the Lord help us to be big enough for his 'all nations'; true enough to his 'all things'; and loyal enough to his 'all authority' to merit the fulfillment of his all-sufficient promise, 'Lo, I am with you alway.' "

May 14, 1919, had been a busy day for Southern Baptists at their sixty-fourth session in Atlanta, Georgia. Dr. J. B. Gambrell had been reelected president and had made his famous address setting forth what he felt to be the Baptist relation to the government and to other denominations. The reports of the Sunday School Board, the Relief and Annuity Board, the Home Mission Board, and the Foreign Mission Board had been heard.

When the time for the annual sermon came on Wednesday night, Dr. M. E. Dodd, pastor of the First Baptist Church of Shreveport, Louisiana, stepped to the pulpit stand and brought a ringing missionary challenge to Southern Baptists which climaxed with the statement quoted above.

The messengers were stirred, and one Virginia pastor presented a resolution calling on Southern Baptists to face the task of world evangelization. The resolution was referred to a committee—and out of that committee report grew the Seventy-five Million Campaign.

This incident in the life of Monroe Elmon Dodd is but one example of the events in Southern Baptist history which he touched in an intimate way.

Monroe Elmon Dodd was born at Brazil, Tennessee, on September 8, 1878, and was brought up on a farm. At the age of seventeen he taught school; but he soon returned to Union University at Jackson, Tennessee, where he was graduated with honors in 1904. Before graduation in April, 1902, he was ordained by the First Church of Trenton, Tennessee.

Upon graduation in 1904, there were two events of importance: First, he was called as pastor at Fulton, Kentucky; a short time later he was married to Emma Savage. They wanted to go to Persia as missionaries; but as that door was closed, they went to Mexico. Unsettled conditions in that country made it impossible to stay, and they returned to Fulton.

In 1912 Dr. Dodd (he received an honorary doctor's degree from several schools, including Baylor University) was called as pastor of the First Baptist Church, Shreveport, where he served for nearly forty years, with the exception of a few months in 1927 when he served the Temple Baptist Church in Los Angeles.

While president of the Southern Baptist Convention, he and Mrs. Dodd made a world mission tour. He also made a tour of many of the mission fields on other trips, traveling most of the time by plane. He presided over a session and addressed the Baptist World Alliance meeting in Berlin in 1934. He was chairman of the committee which recommended that Southern Baptists adopt the Cooperative Program as the method of financing their mission work.

In 1944 Southern Baptists called on Dr. Dodd to lead in a

crusade to win a million souls for Christ in 1945. The final goal was not reached, but a crusade was launched which was climaxed in the simultaneous revivals.

Dr. Dodd retired as active pastor of the Shreveport church in 1950 and died on August 6, 1952.

John R. Sampey
1936-1938

"As I lay on the trundle bed on the night of March 3, 1877, I could not go to sleep. We had just had family prayers, and Father was reading and Mother was knitting. My younger brother had fallen asleep beside me; but I was in distress over my sins. In my desperation I lifted my eyes upward and began to talk in a whisper to the Savior. I said to him: 'Lord Jesus, I do not know what to do. I have prayed, but I get no relief. I have read the Bible, but my sins are still a burden on my soul. I have listened to preaching, but find no help. I do not know what to do except to turn it all over to you; and if I am lost, I will go down trusting you.' "

John Richard Sampey never got away from his conversion experience. He told it, with tears of joy running down his cheeks on hundred of occasions. He repeated it in his *Memoirs*. It became the dynamic for a great life dedicated to preaching and teaching.

John Richard Sampey was born at Fort Deposit, Alabama, September 27, 1863. His father had been a Methodist preacher, but as he read his Bible he had become convinced that the Baptist position was more in accord with New Testament teachings. He had joined a Baptist church and had been ordained as a Baptist minister.

Young John was licensed to preach when he was fifteen. He was graduated from Howard College (now Samford University) with highest honors and then completed his graduate course at Southern Baptist Seminary in 1885.

Dr. Sampey remained at the Louisville seminary as teacher and president for more than half a century. During his tenure as teacher, he taught Hebrew and Old Testament to more students than had any other teacher. Because of his ability to make the characters of the Old Testament live and was especially effective in describing the founder of the Assyrian Empire, he was called "Tiglath-pileser" by his students. He was known affectionately as "Old Tig."

When Dr. E. Y. Mullins died in November 1928, Dr. Sampey was named as the acting president of Southern Seminary; he became president in May 1929. He served in this capacity until he retired from active duty in 1942.

Dr. Sampey will be best remembered, perhaps, as a teacher and seminary president; but he made contributions in many other areas. He served as a pastor of churches near Louisville. He made a real contribution to the Christian life in South America and China through his evangelistic tours. He succeeded the late John A. Broadus as a member of the International Uniform Sunday School Lesson Committee, serving for forty-six years in that work. He was president of the Southern Baptist Convention from 1936 to 1938.

Dr. Sampey passed away Sunday afternoon, August 8, 1946. Funeral services were conducted by Dr. Ellis Fuller in the Crescent Hill Baptist Church, Louisville. At Dr. Sampey's request, no reference was made to him or to his work at his funeral. Dr. Sampey had asked that the time be taken in reading the Scriptures and telling of the goodness of Jesus.

L. R. Scarborough
1939-1940

"I charge thee in the sight of God, and of Christ Jesus, who shall judge the living and the dead, and by his appearing and his kingdom: preach the Word. . . ."

The day was April 11, 1945. The place was the chapel of the Southwestern Baptist Theological Seminary. The reader was Dr. Jeff D. Ray, veteran professor. The occasion was the funeral of Dr. Lee Rutland Scarborough. This text from the fourth chapter of Paul's second letter to Timothy had been the text of Dr. Scarborough's life: "Preach the Word."

Lee Rutland Scarborough was born in Colfax, Louisiana, July 4, 1870. When he was four years of age, the family moved to Texas.

Although Lee made a profession of faith at the age of fourteen and joined a Baptist church, he did not feel that he had been converted. It was not until three years later, in a Presbyterian revival, that he gave his life to Christ. He was not baptized then, but he could not get the matter off his mind; so while a student in Baylor University, he asked to be baptized by the First Baptist Church of Waco by Dr. B. H. Carroll.

When Lee was graduated from Baylor, his parents and many of his friends prayed that he would go on to the seminary and train for the ministry. But the young man was interested in law, and he went to Yale to take graduate work in law. However before the end of the first year he wrote his mother. "I have surrendered to preach. Please show this letter to my father."

In 1899 Lee Scarborough attended the Southern Baptist Theological Seminary, but the death of his brother brought his formal education to an end.

In 1908 Dr. B. H. Carroll persuaded Dr. Scarborough to leave a successful pastorate at Abilene, Texas, to build a "chair of fire"—evangelism—at Southwestern Seminary. Succeeding Dr. Carroll as president in 1916, he served in that capacity until he retired in 1942. Following Dr. Scarborough's example, hundreds of young men have gone out to "preach the Word" with evangelistic fervor.

As director of the Seventy-five Million Campaign, Dr. Scarborough literally gave his very heart and life to Southern Baptists and to the cause of Christ around the world. In addition to serving as president of the Texas Baptist Convention and of the Southern Baptist Convention, he was elected vice-president of the Baptist World Alliance in 1940.

One of the most interesting stories told about the life of Lee Scarborough is that of "The House That Was Never Built." His parents lived in a small, poorly-equipped ranch house; and it was their dream someday to build a better house. They sacrificed and saved for it. When Lee was sixteen years of age, they felt that they had enough money to build their dream home and began to make their final plans.

But when Mr. Scarborough took his wife to see the beautiful site he had selected, she turned to her husband, her eyes filled with tears, and said, "My dear, I do appreciate your desire to build me a new, comfortable home upon this place of beauty; but there is another call for our money which is far greater. Let's live on in the old house and use this money we have saved to send Lee to college."

Because that house was never built, his biographer, H. E. Dana, tells us, other houses for the education of youth, hospitals for the sick, and houses of worship and soul-winning were built through the efforts of that son.

At the dedication of beautiful Scarborough Hall at Southwestern Seminary on February 8, 1950, Dr. C. E. Matthews said that "simplicity of speech, sincerity of purpose, and human approach to man were the three great qualities of Dr. Scarborough. . . . He was a natural leader of men, standing out in any crowd. He knew no fear save the fear of God." In closing, Dr. Matthews said that Dr. Scarborough is "now living in two worlds—in this one through his influence and in the other in person." Appropriately enough, a memento which Mrs. Scarborough chose to place in the cornerstone was a copy of *With Christ After the Lost,* a text used by Dr. Scarborough when he taught the course in evangelism at Southwestern Seminary.

W. W. Hamilton
1941-1942

World conditions looked dark on June 13, 1940, when
President L. R. Scarborough called the morning session of the
eighty-fifth meeting of the Southern Baptist Convention to
order in Baltimore.

The morning headlines told of the entry into Paris by the
victorious German army. The British had saved most of their
forces at Dunkirk but had been forced from the Continent
and lay almost undefended. Italy had declared war on the
Allies in order to share the spoils.

Times were tense. Thoughts of war were expressed from
the platform. Messengers thought of sons and loved ones as
they sat in the steamy old Baltimore Armory where the
meetings were being held.

As a break came in the morning program before the report
of the Executive Committee which was to call for "A Debt-
Free Denomination in 1945," a white-haired man slipped
quietly to the microphone on the platform and moved "that
the evangelistic emphasis of the Southern Baptist Convention
so blessed of God for these past two years, be renewed and

56

continued for this next Convention year."

The motion was carried, and it was no surprise when the time for the election of officers came that afternoon, that Robert H. Coleman nominated the same quiet, dignified man for president of the Southern Baptist Convention. This William Wistar Hamilton, then president of the Baptist Bible Institute, became the twenty-second president of the Southern Baptist Convention.

The Convention in Baltimore made its first protest against the sending of a representative to the Vatican; and it politely, but firmly, declined the invitation to join the World Council of Churches. The messengers agreed with Dr. Hamilton that the answer did not lie in a big church, either Roman or Protestant, wielding a big stick, but it was to be found in the humble but zealous witness of the individual Christian.

W. W. Hamilton was born in Christian County, Kentucky, December 9, 1868. He attended King College in Bristol, Tennessee, and then went on to the Southern Baptist Seminary where he completed his work in 1904. He was ordained in 1893 in the First Church, Bristol, Tennessee.

After pastorates in Virginia, West Virginia, and Kentucky, Dr. Hamilton was elected superintendent of evangelism for the Home Mission Board and served from 1906 until 1909. After a nine-year pastorate at Lynchburg, Virginia, he returned to the Home Mission Board in 1918. In 1922 Dr. Hamilton went to the St. Charles Avenue Church in New Orleans and served there until 1928, when he was elected president of the Baptist Bible Institute (now New Orleans Baptist Theological Seminary). During his years there he led that school to become a vital center of evangelism.

In 1943 Dr. Hamilton became pastor of the Gentilly Street Church in New Orleans. He was chaplain of the New Orleans Hospital for several years before his death on November 19, 1960.

Pat M. Neff
1944-1946

Three men who have served as president of the Southern Baptist Convention have also served as governor of the states in which they lived. The first was W. J. Northen of Georgia. The second was James P. Eagle of Arkansas. Pat Morris Neff of Texas was the third.

When the Southern Baptist Convention met in San Antonio, Texas, in May 1942, the feeling was expressed by many messengers that it was time for a layman to serve as president again. It had been more than thirty years since Joshua Levering, another great Christian layman, had served. When the time for nominating a president arrived, E. D. Solomon of Florida and J. M. Dawson of Texas both hurried to the speaker's stand. President Hamilton recognized Dr. Solomon, who nominated Pat Morris Neff. Dr. Dawson, with the same purpose, had to be content with seconding the nomination. Without other nominations, Pat Neff was unanimously elected.

Pat Morris Neff was born at McGregor, Texas, November 28, 1871. He received his bachelor of arts degree from Baylor

58

University in 1894 and then went on to the University of Texas, where he received his law degree in 1897. Among his classmates at the university were the late Senator Morris Sheppard and Senator Tom Connally, chairman of the Foreign Relations Committee. He then returned to Baylor where he received his master's degree in 1898. His classmates at Baylor included the late Samuel Palmer Brooks and George W. Truett.

After graduation he opened his practice of law in Waco and gained distinction as a legislator and as a prosecuting attorney. In 1921 he was elected governor of Texas and served for two terms. From 1927 to 1929 he served as a member of the United States Board of Mediation, and then for two years he was chairman of the Texas Railroad Commission.

For more than a quarter of a century he served as president of the board of trustees of Baylor University. It is significant that in 1931 the trustees turned to him as president to succeed Dr. Brooks, who had died during the year. Pat Neff served as president of Baylor until his retirement in 1947. The university saw its greatest period of building and expansion under his fifteen years of service.

Serving as president was no new experience for Pat Neff who had served as president of the Texas Baptist Convention and in 1933 he had been elected vice-president of the Southern Baptist Convention. He encouraged the messengers to feel that discussion was open to all, and the number of messengers participating in the discussions greatly increased during his tenure.

Pat Neff believed in Baptists—and, above all, believed in God. In 1943, when the Convention had to be deferred because of the war, he wrote, "In these troublous days when the foundations of the world are shaken and nations are torn asunder with war and death, let every Southern Baptist attune his soul to the call of the still small Voice to 'be strong in the Lord, and in the power of his might.' Let us with all courage and undiminishing zeal go on with the work which has been committed to us. While we walk in the midst of tribulation and the shadows of destruction lengthen upon the earth, we can yet trust in him who created man in his own image; we can depend upon him to lead us out of the darkness; we can 'sail ahead, and leave the rest to God.' "

Dr. Neff died in Waco, Texas, on January 20, 1952.

Louie D. Newton
1947-1948

April 20, 1929, stands out as an eventful day in the history of old Union Baptist Church in the Middle Association of Georgia—for that was the day when seventy-five of the leading ministers of the state crowded into the Screven County rural church for the ordination of one of her illustrious sons, Louie Devotie Newton.

On the hot, summer day in July 1902, when Louie D. Newton was baptized in a nearby stream, the ten-year-old farm boy had little idea that someday he would return to be ordained to the ministry by that same church. He was more concerned about his duties on the farm and his studies in the one-room country school.

After completing the community school, Louie went to a boarding school and then on to Mercer University, where he was graduated in 1913. Elected to the faculty on the day of his graduation, he taught during the regular term and worked on his master's degree at Columbia University in the summers. It was while he was in New York that he developed his interest in journalism. He received his M.A. degree in 1915.

Another event of importance in 1915 was his marriage to Julia Winn Carstarphen of Macon.

Young Newton was just settling down as a professor of history at Mercer when World War I interrupted his career. He shifted his interests to serve as director of the educational activities of the National War Work Council at Camp Wheeler until the armistice.

At this time Southern Baptists were launching the Seventy-five Million Campaign, and Louie D. Newton was drafted to serve as director of publicity for Georgia. Because of his work, it was natural for Georgia Baptists to select him as editor when the state board voted to buy the *Christian Index* from private interests in December 1919.

If the *Christian Index* ranked as first love during the next decade, then it can be said that the Druid Hills Baptist Church ranked a close second. The church was expanding during this period under the leadership of the eloquent F. C. McConnell. Louie D. Newton served as chairman of the deacons and teacher of the Men's Class during this period of building and growth.

When Dr. McConnell died on January 12,1929, the pulpit committee petitioned Dr. Newton to accept the pastorate. He replied that he was a layman and could not accept the invitation. Again he was elected, but he declined. When the third invitation came, he could not escape the conviction that God's hand was evident; and he accepted on March 27, 1929, with the understanding that Druid Hills would ask his old home church, where his mother and father still held their membership, to ordain him to the ministry.

He was elected as president of the Southern Baptist Convention in Miami in 1946 and was reelected at the Southern Baptist Convention in St. Louis. He was a longtime member of the Executive Committee of the Southern Baptist Convention, the Georgia Baptist Convention, and the Baptist World Alliance.

He has served two years as president of the Georgia Baptist Convention and has been named as one of the vice-presidents of the Baptist World Alliance.

Like his father, Dr. Newton is still interested in farming. His hobbies are caring for his two-acre patch, his chickens, his flowers, and fishing.

Robert G. Lee
1949-1951

"I introduce to you Naboth. Naboth was a devout Israelite who lived in the foothill village of Jezreel. Naboth was a good man. He abhorred that which is evil and clave to that which is good. . . ." It was at the prayer meeting time on a Wednesday night back in 1919 at the historic old Baptist church in Edgefield, South Carolina, that these now-famous words were first spoken.

"Say, pastor! I sorta liked that talk you gave tonight," a deacon is said to have commented as he left the building. "Why don't you make a full-length sermon out of it?"

Robert Greene Lee did make a full-length sermon out of it—and thus was born the famous sermon "Pay Day—Some Day," which has been heard by perhaps more than a million people in the more than four hundred times it has been preached since 1919.

Robert G. Lee will be remembered by many as a helpful pastor and counselor. He will be remembered by many young people as a friend in time of need. He will be remembered by many as a denominational statesman who had enough knowledge of Baptist history to give him a vision of the Baptist future. But Dr. R. G. Lee will be remembered above all, perhaps, as a zealous, evangelistic preacher.

Convictions come out of vital experiences, and Dr. R. G. Lee has had his share. From that cool morning of November 11, 1886, when the fifth child arrived in the log cabin of David Ayers Lee and Sarah Bennett Lee, sharecroppers in York County, South Carolina, his has been no easy task.

Just before young Lee was twelve years of age, he accepted Jesus as Savior and on August 5, 1898, was baptized into the fellowship of the First Baptist Church of Fort Mill, South Carolina. Almost from the beginning of his Christian experience, he felt the desire to preach. He worked on the farm until he was twenty-one and did not have much opportunity to go to school during that period. But the burning fire was still in his heart.

At the age of twenty-one, he went to Panama to work on the canal and try to earn enough money to enter Furman University. He gained more experience than money; but he did enter Furman upon his return, even though he had to take one year of preparatory work before entering college. When the young man completed his college work, he had not only won the coveted gold medal for the best oration, but he also won the heart of Miss Bula Gentry. They were married on November 26, 1913.

The young couple served South Carolina rural churches until 1918, when Robert Lee was called as pastor of the Edgefield Church in South Carolina. There followed pastorates at Chester, South Carolina; New Orleans, Louisiana; and Charleston, South Carolina, before Dr. Lee preached his first sermon at Bellevue Baptist Church, Memphis, on December 11, 1927. He was pastor there until his retirement in 1960.

Dr. Lee served as president of the Tennessee Baptist Convention from 1932 to 1935. He was elected president of the

Southern Baptist Convention at Memphis in 1948 and again at Oklahoma City in 1949. Tradition had developed that a man should be elected for only two terms, but when the Convention met in Chicago in May 1950, and the time for nominations came, there was only one nomination—and the name was Robert Greene Lee.

Southern Baptists felt that he was God's man for God's hour.

J. D. Grey
1952-1953

Football fans from all sections of the United States filled the mammoth Sugar Bowl stadium at New Orleans on January 1, 1951, for the annual Sugar Bowl classic, featuring the teams from the University of Oklahoma and the University of Kentucky.

It was not a religious gathering. The game was being played in a great Catholic city. Suddenly an announcement came from the loud speaker and the yelling fans stopped their noise and stood with heads bowed. A Baptist preacher, Dr. J. D. Grey, pastor of the First Baptist Church of New Orleans, was called to lead in prayer.

This little incident from the life of the president of the Southern Baptist Convention gives some indication of the impact he has made on the city of New Orleans.

James David Grey was born at Princeton, Kentucky, December 18, 1906. A few years later his parents moved to Paducah, Kentucky, and became members of the old Second Baptist Church.

When J. D. was twelve years old, Dr. John W. P. Givens

assisted Pastor H. W. Ellis in a revival meeting. One night as the evangelist preached on the penitent thief, a twelve-year-old boy made his way up the aisle, and, in answer to the prayers of his mother and a concerned Sunday School teacher, J. D. Grey made his profession of faith in Jesus Christ as Lord and Savior.

Six years later, while a senior in high school, J. D. was to deliver his first sermon in the same church where he had accepted Christ. He soon entered Union University and there became a close friend to Dr. I. N. Penick, the professor of Bible. Dr. Grey can remember now hearing Dr. Penick say time and time again, speaking of the Bible, "Brethren, whet your Jerusalem blade and go down to battle."

After completing his work at Union University in 1929, J. D. entered the Southwestern Baptist Theological Seminary; he received his Th.M. degree from that institution in 1932. He was honored by his alma mater, Union University, with a doctor of divinity degree in 1938.

Dr. Grey pays tribute to several preachers who have influenced his life and ministry. When he was just sixteen years of age, a fellow Kentuckian, Dr. M. E. Dodd, invited J. D. to visit the First Baptist Church, Shreveport, Louisiana, at the time of the dedication of their new building and had him stay in his home. He never got away from that experience, and twelve years later he had one of the greatest thrills of his life when he returned to the First Baptist Church, Shreveport, to supply the pulpit for Dr. Dodd. He also pays tribute to Dr. L. R. Scarborough, who helped him in many ways during his seminary experience; and to Dr. George W. Truett, who encouraged him as a young preacher.

Since completing his seminary work in 1932, Dr. Grey has served in only three churches. He served as pastor of Tabernacle Baptist Church, Ennis, Texas, until 1934; he was pastor of First Baptist Church, Denton, Texas, from 1934 to 1937;

and he was pastor of the First Baptist Church, New Orleans, from 1937 until his retirement in December, 1972.

Before he completed his work at Union University, J. D. Grey married his Paducah sweetheart, Lillian Gaines Tooke, on September 16, 1927. They have twin daughters, Mary Beth and Martha Ann, born September 3, 1941.

Dr. Grey, who is the youngest man ever elected as president of the Southern Baptist Convention, is an informal person. As he recently stated, "I delight to call people by their given names and feel honored when they do the same for me. I have always felt especially close to the men of my church and community. I have always been rather happy somehow in the thought that I was a man before I was a preacher."

In addition to his service as president of the Southern Baptist Convention, he has served as vice-president of the Southern Baptist Convention, as president of the Louisiana Baptist Convention; as president of the alumni of Southwestern Baptist Seminary; as a member of the Executive Committee of the Baptist World Alliance; as a member of the Home Mission Board; and as a "Baptist Hour" preacher in April, May, and June 1949.

J. W. Storer
1954-1955

A twenty-one-year-old cowboy tucked one trouser leg in his boot, saddled his horse, and headed for Baker, Oregon, ten miles away, to listen to the verbal fight he had heard was brewing between the Baptists and the Seventh-Day Adventists.

Calvary Baptist Church was lighted up for the meeting, and the crowd was expecting fireworks. The Adventists did not appear, but James Wilson Storer stayed to enjoy the music. He soon found himself thrilled by the most wonderful story he had ever heard.

On the following night the young cowboy returned to the little Baptist church. When the invitation was given, he surrendered his life to Christ. After studying his Bible for several weeks, he asked to be baptized into the membership of that church.

Jim Storer put the same enthusiasm into his life as a Christian that he had shown on the range. In a few weeks he was elected Sunday School superintendent. After several conferences with his pastor, Harry Secor, he asked the church to license him to preach.

He planned to enter Bucknell College, a Baptist school in Pennsylvania; but on the trip East he stopped in Kansas, where he had been born on December 1, 1886. There someone told him about William Jewell College in Missouri. Since his train did not leave until that night, Jim Storer went to Liberty; and President J. P. Green convinced him that William Jewell was "the only Baptist college in America."

Jim Storer made such fast progress at William Jewell that he completed grade school, high school, and college work in six years. He adds, with a twinkle in his eye, that the most important event was meeting Miss Nora Isabel Wilbanks.

At William Jewell, Storer developed a deep interest in and appreciation for the Bible, good music, history, and literature. He considered the degree he received there in 1912 as a hunting license for continued study. He received honorary degrees from Union University, Oklahoma Baptist University, and William Jewell College.

After his graduation, Storer was called as pastor at Watonga, Oklahoma, with a salary of $900 per year. The young pastor coached basketball and baseball to supplement his income; and he needed more income because Miss Wilbanks, then librarian at Stephens College in Missouri, became Mrs. Storer that December.

After a year as pastor at Pauls Valley, he served at Ripley, Tennessee; Paris, Tennessee; Greenwood, Mississippi; and Richmond, Virginia, before accepting the call of the First Baptist Church, Tulsa, Oklahoma, on October 1, 1931. After his retirement, he was elected executive secretary of the Southern Baptist Foundation on November 1, 1956.

Dr. James Wilson Storer was the ideal for many young men. He commanded the love, admiration, and respect of his fellow ministers. This confidence was shown in his election to head many important committees; to serve on the Foreign Mission Board; to serve as president of the Oklahoma Baptist Convention and as president of the trustees of Oklahoma Baptist University; to serve as a member of the Executive Committee of the Southern Baptist Convention for many years, and as president of the Convention.

Dr. Storer has often been called a "preacher's preacher," and many of his reflections on the ministry are to be found in his book published by the Broadman Press: *The Preacher: His Belief and Behavior*. He had a keen sense of humor, but also a keen sense of the urgency of his task.

A part of his philosophy may be found in these re-Storertives:

"Major on Christian affirmations. These are not the days for apologetic uncertainties in things pertaining to the souls of men and God's grace in their behalf."

"Do not stifle your sense of humor—it is a pledge of sanity in the ministry. But keep it under control—a buffoon in the pulpit is an abomination to God and man."

"Do not preach too long; it is easier to be prolix than it is to be proficient; the nearer empty is a fountain pen, the faster it runs. And remember, you can always tell what kind of wheels are in a man's head by the spokes that come out of his mouth."

"Read widely, but wisely. Never bother with the 'book of the month'—usually a month is all it lasts. Ahead of all books—know your Bible."

Dr. Storer died in Nashville, Tennessee, on April 12, 1970.

C. C. Warren
1956-1957

The charred remains of three little bodies were found in the ashes of a burned tenant house about three miles out from Danville, Kentucky.

A young pastor, who had rushed to the scene after hearing of the tragedy, joined the forty or fifty friends standing around the smoking ruins to bring what comfort he could to the bereaved parents.

"Who is their pastor?" he inquired.

"They ain't got no pastor, Mister. They ain't got no church. They're just poor tenant farmers."

That reply burned hotter than the embers of the fire into the heart of the young pastor. On Sunday morning as he unburdened his heart at the First Baptist Church in Danville, there came a response on the part of the church to see that church facilities were provided for the people of that community.

A church census in the area showed five hundred prospects, and soon a thriving mission was launched. Other missions were started in other localities, and that course of action eventually brought recognition from the Southern Baptist Convention with the election of Casper Carl Warren as its president.

C. C. Warren laughingly says that he was born in a huckleberry patch of Starling Swamp just below Mingo, in Sampson, North Carolina, three miles northeast of Spring Branch. The date was May 28, 1896. The mother was Rosella Strickland Warren; and the father was Richard Moore Warren, a Sampson County farmer.

Dr. Warren was one of eight children. Among the never-to-be-forgotten impressions of his childhood were the reading of the Bible in the home and the devotion to the little country church and to the Christ of his mother and his deacon father.

Young Warren was a student in Wake Forest College when World War I interrupted his education, and he served as an officer in the artillery until the armistice. He then went back to Wake Forest and obtained his law degree in 1920.

For more than two years he practiced law in Dunn, North Carolina, and was building up a profitable practice. He found, however, that his interest in the work at the church was greater than his interest in his law practice. He was superintendent of his Sunday School, and it became the first Advanced Sunday School in the South. He was president of the North Carolina B.Y.P.U. He wrote articles on Sunday School work. He received many invitations to speak. He was offered opportunities to become an educational director.

Over a twelve-month period Casper Warren fought the battle through. Then, on a Saturday afternoon in September, he wrote out his resignation as superintendent of the Sunday School and caught a train for Louisville to attend the Southern Baptist Theological Seminary.

As the train pulled into Frankfort, Kentucky, another young ministerial student, who had been one of Casper's roommates at Wake Forest, got on the train. Forrest Feezor remembers to this day that he did not have to be told what had happened. It was Feezor, state mission secretary in Texas, who nominated Warren for president of the Southern Baptist Convention.

Shortly after reaching Louisville, Casper Warren met Miss Mary Strickland of Danville, Virginia, a student in the WMU Training School, who had given her life for definite Christian service. She did not know what that service would be; but on August 26, 1925, she decided that it would be as a pastor's wife. The Warrens had three children.

During his stay in the seminary, Casper Warren served as assistant pastor at West Broadway and at Deer Park churches, and later, as pastor at Evergreen, a rural church. He served as assistant to Dr. A. T. Robertson during the three years before he received his Th.D. in 1928.

After completing his seminary work, Dr. Warren served in only three pastorates. The first was at Danville, Kentucky, where he stayed for ten and a half years and found his love for developing mission churches.

The second pastorate was at the Immanuel Church in Little Rock, Arkansas, where the concern for mission churches developed and grew. The third was as pastor of the First Baptist Church, Charlotte, North Carolina, where he stayed until he was selected to head up the 30,000 Movement. He died in Charlotte, North Carolina, on May 20, 1973. He was responsible, as much as any one man, for the launching of the Baptist Jubilee Advance.

Brooks Hays
1958-1959

A thirty-five-year-old young man had twice been the runner-up in the race for governor in the state of Arkansas. Now, facing a court test in a very close race for a seat in the United States Congress, he sat in the courtroom where the final decision would be handed down, involving the lawsuit over the contested seat.

"On the personal side," he says, "the court decision meant the obliteration of my investment in public life—the denial of an office I had finally won. In this mood I sat down on the fateful morning in a beautiful, walnut-paneled courtroom to hear the judge deliver what I knew would be a ruling against me. I prayed. It might be more accurate to say that I talked with God. I asked him not to desert me. I felt that he was on my side.

"Here was suffering which was doubly bitter because it was unjust," he adds, "but I did not want to be embittered or to develop cynicism toward the political system or the people embraced by it. I asked God to save me from it. I felt, at the moment, that he was answering my prayer. The assurance I had as my case was dismissed—that nothing could hurt me if I was not hurt inside—was a complete one, and I walked out of the room as calm and unperturbed as I have ever been in my life."

That feeling of the presence of God is one thing that has characterized the life of Brooks Hays, who was elected president of the Southern Baptist Convention in 1957. He was the sixth layman to be elected to that office and the twenty-ninth man to be elected president in the one hundred and twelve years of the Southern Baptist Convention's history.

Brooks Hays believes in prayer; and at the meeting of the Executive Committee, in one of the first statements he made after he was elected, he pledged himself to a program of increased prayer and Bible study.

However, President Hays did not believe in exploiting religion for his own point of view. He says: "I determined early in my own career that I would not identify my candidacy with a 'righteous cause.' This is not to say that, from the standpoint of moral values, political campaigns do not present clear choices. In most races 'the right' is distinguishable as favoring one side over the other. I am pointing out, however, that invoking divine approbation for the purpose of gaining favor at the polls is not in our tradition and should be repudiated, and I believe it generally will be. I believe strongly in the practice of prayer in political matters, but I question the use of prayer for victory for oneself or a favorite."

Brooks Hays was born near Russellville, Arkansas, on August 9, 1898. His mother and father were active members of a Baptist church, and it was only natural that Brooks Hays should accept Jesus Christ as Lord and Savior at the age of eleven. He reveals, however, that despite his Baptist upbringing, he was converted at a Methodist revival meeting. "I had accompanied my grandmother, who was a Methodist, to the meeting," the former Congressman recalls. "The preacher was the Rev. Joe Ramsey, a Mississippian, who was totally blind. He was one of the most eloquent speakers I've ever heard."

Through some misunderstanding, the young Hays was taken into the Methodist church; but the next Sunday things were all straightened out, and he was duly received as a candidate for baptism in the Baptist church.

Brooks Hays recalls that one of his first speaking experiences was in the old B.Y.P.U., and he recalls that out of that experience grew a tension in his own life as to whether he should become a minister or should follow his father in the field of law and politics. He prayed the matter through, and the decision came clearly to him that he ought to make a Christian witness in the legal profession and in the field of politics.

He attended the public schools in Russellville. He received his A.B. degree from the University of Arkansas and his LL.B. degree from George Washington University Law School.

Sharing in his interest as president of the Convention was his wife, who taught the Burrell Sunday School Class in the Calvary Baptist Church, Washington, D. C. Mrs. Hays was Marian Prather of Fort Smith, Arkansas, until she said yes to the handsome young lawyer in 1922.

Mr. Hays was elected to Congress to represent the Fifth (Little Rock) District in 1942 and was reelected every two years until 1958. In 1955 he was named as a member of the United States Delegation to the General Assembly of the United Nations. He served on the staff at the White House under both President Eisenhower and President Kennedy. He also served as a member of the Board of the Tennessee Valley Authority.

Denominational service was nothing new to Brooks Hays. As a young man, he was superintendent of the Sunday School of the First Baptist Church, Russellville, and then chairman of the deacons of the Second Baptist Church, Russellville; he has been a teacher of a men's class in the Second Baptist Church, Little Rock, where he now attends when he is in that city. He is honored as "a member of the congregation" of the Calvary Baptist Church, in Washington, D. C. Incidentally, the president of the American Baptist Convention that same year, 1958, was Dr. Clarence W. Cranford, the pastor of Calvary Baptist Church.

Mr. Hays served as the chairman of the Arkansas Baptist Rural Church Commission, as a member of the Executive Board of the Arkansas Baptist Convention, as president of the Arkansas Children's Home board, as chairman of the Christian Life Commission, and in 1951 as vice-president of the Southern Baptist Convention.

Ramsey Pollard
1960-1961

An eleven-year-old Junior boy sat in the balcony of the First Baptist Church in Amarillo, Texas, during a revival meeting held by the pastor, Dr. Wallace Bassett.

When the invitation was given, a tall, big-shouldered Sunday School teacher came and put his hand on the shoulder of this Junior boy and asked the question, "Ramsey, are you ready to give your heart to Jesus?"

The eleven-year-old boy, who was seated with his Junior friends, was somewhat embarrassed by the question; and he quickly ducked behind the excuse that he didn't have on his coat and he wanted to wait until he had on a coat to go down the aisle. The interested Sunday School teacher, whose heart was as big as his body, offered, with a twinkle in his eye, the loan of his coat. That act pierced the heart of Ramsey Pollard, and he made his way to the front under the protecting care of the big hand of his Sunday School teacher placed lovingly on his shoulder.

Ramsey Pollard was born February 15, 1903, in Cleburne, Texas, the son of Mr and Mrs. B. O. Pollard. Mr. Pollard was

80

a pioneer police officer in central Texas.

A few years after Ramsey Pollard's conversion experience, Dr. Bassett accepted the call of the Cliff Temple Baptist Church in Dallas, Texas; and Dr. H. W. Virgin became pastor of the Amarillo church. Young Ramsey dated Isabel, the youngest daughter of Dr. and Mrs. Virgin. One starlit night when they were sitting on the front porch of the Virgin home, her father's voice boomed out, asking the young caller to come upstairs to his office. Fear seized young Ramsey; and he was disturbed when he entered the study door and the pastor said bluntly, "Ramsey, I believe God wants you to be a preacher."

The Pollards soon moved to Dallas, and again Dr. Bassett was their pastor. Ramsey taught a Sunday School class and was very active in the B.Y.P.U. He also met Della Pickle, who, on June 9, 1923, became Mrs. Ramsey Pollard.

Ramsey and his bride moved to Florida, where the young man was working at the Citizens Bank and Trust Company in Tampa. Then one of the deacons of the El Bethel Baptist Church asked if he would supply the next Sunday. As Mr. Pollard prepared for that sermon, he came face to face with the call he had been fighting for many years, and he felt that God wanted him to give his full time to the ministry. He was ordained on December 16, 1925. After serving as pastor for nearly five years, he resigned to enter the Southwestern Baptist Theological Seminary in Fort Worth, Texas.

During the period that Mr. Pollard was in the seminary, he served as pastor of the First Baptist Church, Handley, Texas, and of the Evans Avenue Baptist Church in Fort Worth. In 1939 he was called as pastor of the Broadway Church in Knoxville, Tennessee, where he served for twenty years. He accepted the call of the Bellevue Baptist Church in Memphis in January 1960, and stayed until retirement in June 1972.

Dr. Pollard does not consider himself a religious statesman but prefers to be known as a preacher and evangelist. In the

Convention sermon which he preached at the Southern Baptist Convention in Miami in 1952 he said: "The curse of modern-day preaching is the shameful lack of compassion. Too many preachers are calm expositors of truth rather than impassioned preachers of the gospel. We have allowed ourselves to be laughed out of our enthusiasm. We have let the devil convince us that, if compassion and zeal are elements in our preaching, some highbrow will point the finger of scorn and contempt in our direction and pronounce that we are emotional, and therefore lacking in intelligence.

"There is no conflict," Dr. Pollard continued, "between intelligence and emotion. Paul had both; and, if we are to be worthy witnesses for Christ, we must have something to say, and we must deliver our souls with compassion and zeal."

Serving as president of a distinguished body was no completely new experience for the thirtieth president of the Southern Baptist Convention. Dr. Pollard served as president of the Southern Baptist Convention Pastors' Conference, as president of the Tennessee Baptist Convention, as chairman of the Radio and Television Commission, and as chairman of the Executive Committee of the Southern Baptist Convention. He was honored with an honorary Doctor of Divinity degree from Carson-Newman College and another honorary degree from Atlanta Law School.

The Pollards have two children, Ramsey, Jr., and Imogene, who is now Mrs. Robert Cliett. The Pollards also have four grandchildren.

Herschel H. Hobbs
1962-1963

Elbert Oscar Hobbs sold his little hardware business in Talladega, Alabama, in 1900. He and his wife planned to purchase a new business in Oklahoma City, which was a thriving, newborn city on the Western Plains in Indian Territory. Just as the family was getting ready to move, the doctor advised Elbert Hobbs not to go to the western climate but to move to a farm in Alabama.

Elbert Hobbs was never to see Oklahoma, for he passed away in 1910. His son, Herschel Harold Hobbs, was born on the 685-acre Coosa County farm near Talladega Springs on October 24, 1907. Herschel was later to become pastor of the First Baptist Church in Oklahoma City and the thirty-second man to serve as president of the Southern Baptist Convention.

Because times were hard after the father died, Mrs. Hobbs sold the farm and moved her family to Ashland, Alabama. There they lived until Herschel was nine years old. In 1916 the Hobbs family moved back to a small farm near Montevallo, Alabama, Some of the earliest memories the Southern

Baptist Convention president had are of the struggle he had in trying to plow a forty-acre tract when he was nine years old. He recalls the joy that came to his heart when the farmers from the surrounding area came in their wagons with seed and food and put in a crop for the Hobbs family in one day.

Mrs. Hobbs, Herschel, and the six girls attended the Enon Baptist Church in the open country. The little church had services only once a month, but it always had an "August revival." One summer, the pastor's son, Ernest Davis, a ministerial student at Howard College (now Samford University), came to Enon for the "August revival." In that service Herschel Hobbs responded to the workings of God's Holy Spirit in his heart and made a public profession of his faith. He was baptized in the Montevallo Creek in August 1918.

"I do not remember what the evangelist preached about," Dr. Hobbs says, "but I do recall vividly that when we started singing 'Let Jesus Come into Your Heart,' I knew I must face life's challenge with the power and presence of his Holy Spirit." Dr. Hobbs adds, "One of the things I wanted to do during my period of service as president was to go back again to Enon Baptist Church."

By 1920 several of Herschel's older sisters were working in Birmingham, and the family moved there and joined Southside Baptist Church. When the family moved to another section of Birmingham two years later, Herschel transferred his membership to Ensley Baptist Church along with the other members of the family.

One of the leaders in the B.Y.P.U at Ensley was Agnes Durant (later to become Mrs. Lake Pylant and eventually the first secretary of the Church Recreation Service of the Sunday School Board). She was interested in providing activities for young people which would tie them closer to the church. She planned a Japanese operetta with lanterns and all that go with them. Frances Jackson was the feminine lead. Much to Mrs. Pylant's dismay, the masculine lead came down with a sore throat shortly before the performance; so she recruited Herschel Hobbs to take the part.

"You would never think I could sing," Dr. Hobbs laughs; "but one of my songs was a plea of proposal to Miss Jackson, and her response was affirmative. This was the way I proposed to my wife the first time I ever met her, and she gladly accepted."

Frances Jackson and Herschel Hobbs were married on April 10, 1917. Jerry Marlin, a son, blessed their home on January 15, 1939.

At the time of his marriage, Herschel Hobbs was working in the roundhouse at the Tennessee Coal and Iron Company. Later he started to work for the Drennen Motor Company in Birmingham. He was ordained a deacon by the Brighton Baptist Church in 1927.

H. H. Hobbs first felt the urge to enter full-time religious service in 1923 while Dr. David Gardner was pastor of Ensley Baptist Church. However, his final commitment to study for the ministry did not come until 1929 when he entered Howard College. In three years he had finished Howard. He then went to Southern Baptist Seminary where he received his Th.M. in 1935 and his Ph.D. in May 1938.

After serving in several churches during his seminary years, he was called to Calvary Church in Birmingham in 1938. Then he served the following churches: Clayton Street in Montgomery; First Baptist Church, Alexandria, Louisiana; and Dauphin Way Baptist Church in Mobile. He accepted the call of the First Baptist Church in Oklahoma City in 1949 where he stayed until retirement in March 1973.

Dr. Hobbs served as president of the Oklahoma Baptist Convention, president of the board of trustees of Oklahoma Baptist University, and as chairman of the board of the Baptist Memorial Hospital in Oklahoma City. He became chairman of the pastors' conference after the retirement of Dr. M. E. Dodd. He was later vice-president of the Baptist World Alliance. However, his first love is preaching. His many years as the "Baptist Hour" preacher—as well as his books, addresses, and sermons—mark him as a "preacher's preacher" among Southern Baptists. Known as an expository preacher, he has a deep conviction that there is a need for a return to a deeper study of the Bible.

"I still spend the entire morning in my study trying to understand what the Bible would say to me this day," Dr. Hobbs says.

One of the great personalities Dr. Hobbs remembers in his life is P. L. Harrup, who was a sponsor of an Intermediate Union in Southside Baptist Church in Birmingham. One of the first messages Dr. Hobbs received when he was elected president of the Southern Baptist Convention was a wire from Mr. Harrup.

K. Owen White
1964

"It is my determined purpose to be president of all Southern Baptists, to be fair, and impartial, and to work with others for the glory of God. Above all else, I am concerned that we shall be even more strongly evangelistic and missionary hearted."

The author of these words was Dr. Kenneth Owen White, pastor of the First Baptist Church of Houston, Texas, at the time; president of the Texas Baptist Convention; and thirty-second man to serve as president of the Southern Baptist Convention.

Dr. White is a man of conviction in his theology as well as in his responsibilities as pastor, evangelist, and missionary; but he is one who holds just as firmly that a man can disagree with some of his brethren without being disagreeable. Actually, it was this right to personal conviction that led him to join a Baptist church.

Kenneth Owen White was born August 29, 1902, in London, England. His father was a good Methodist and a physician. When Kenneth was five years old, the family moved from

London to a ranch in western Canada. His father went to Chinook Cove, north of Kemloops in British Columbia, where he served as doctor, dentist, justice of the peace, and postmaster, as well as rancher.

While a young man in western Canada, K. Owen White took an active interest in the life of his small Methodist Church, and it was this interest that prompted his Sunday School teacher to suggest that God could use him in full-time service as a minister. This suggestion was a fast-growing seed in the mind and heart of young Kenneth; and at the age of nineteen, with high school work uncompleted, he enrolled in the Bible Institute of Los Angeles. It was while there that he met Pearl Woodworth of Ocean Beach, California, who later became his wife.

He completed all of his educational requirements and then went to Louisville, Kentucky, where he not only completed his Ph.D. at the Southern Baptist Seminary, but also earned a B.S. degree at the University of Louisville.

Dr. White filled pastorates in Washington, D. C.; Atlanta, Georgia; and Little Rock, Arkansas, before he was called to the First Baptist Church in Houston in 1953. He stayed in Houston until April 1965 when he accepted the call of California Baptists and the Home Mission Board to serve as metropolitan missions coordinator for the Los Angeles area. He retired in 1968.

At the meeting of the Southern Baptist Convention in Kansas City, Dr. White told the experience of his own conversion as a young man working in a sash-and-door factory: "During the service, two of the ladies in the choir had sung; and the recurring theme of their song was this: 'It was for me that Jesus died on the cross of Calvary. . . .' There was no light from heaven; there was no audible voice that spoke. There was no earthquake. There was no feeling of an electric current playing through my being.

"I was alone," Dr. White said, "just weeping and praying

in the darkness; but there came to me a conviction that I could not shake off, that, if I made this decision and took this step, it would be necessary to give personal testimony to those godless, profane men with whom I worked in the shop. This was hard for me; in fact, it looked almost insurmountable. But, I prayed for strength to do it. I have had to pray for strength many times since that day."

W. Wayne Dehoney
1965-1966

A redheaded, freckled-face boy stood looking at a crack in the floor in the educational building of the First Baptist Church in Oklahoma City.

"This matter of a Christian decision is something each boy must decide for himself," a young lady had explained to the boys who had come for a Royal Ambassador meeting. "I would like for those of you who have accepted Jesus Christ as Savior to come on this side of the crack and those who have not made that decision to stay on the other side."

As Wayne Dehoney, the thirty-third man to serve as president of the Southern Baptist Convention, looked back on that experience, he recalled vividly the leader's explanation of how to become a Christian. As he looked at the crack, he felt the definite conviction that he had the faith to accept that salvation. When his pastor, M. R. Ham, issued the invitation at the close of the next preaching service, nine-year-old Wayne walked down the aisle. He was baptized into the membership of the First Baptist Church, Oklahoma City.

Wayne Dehoney was born in New Raymer, Colorado, on

August 28, 1918. His parents, Mr. and Mrs. W. W. Dehoney, had gone there to farm some of the last homestead land available in Colorado. His parents found more opportunities in teaching than for farming in the dry land of Colorado. Before long, they moved to Cheyenne, Wyoming, for a short period and finally to Oklahoma City, where Mr. Dehoney was a teacher of manual training at the Central High School. Young Wayne finished grade school, junior high school, and the first year of high school in Oklahoma City.

Soon after the young redhead's conversion, Dr. Ham left and Dr. T. L. Holcomb came as the pastor of the First Baptist Church in Oklahoma City. Dr. Holcomb took a personal interest in the three Dehoney brothers and encouraged them in Christian service. (Eugene now operates a feed mill in Twin Falls, Idaho; and Homer is a pilot for American Airlines in Nashville, Tennessee.) Wayne became a good friend of Dr. Holcomb's son Luther, and they dreamed together of the time they could go into law and politics.

When Wayne was a high school sophomore, the family moved to Nashville, where the father was engaged in sales. After Wayne finished Isaac Litton High School in 1936, he entered Vanderbilt University for his prelaw course.

During Wayne's sophomore year at Vanderbilt, his friend Luther Holcomb abandoned his study of law and surrendered for the ministry. Shortly afterward, at the Southwide Student Retreat in Memphis, while debating the question with himself in a hotel room, Wayne Dehoney also felt God's call to give his life to the preaching ministry. He kept the matter to himself until he returned home. Then he talked with his pastor, Dr. W. F. Powell, about his decision. Dr. Powell urged him to make it public on the following Sunday, which he did.

The next year Wayne went to Baylor University in Waco, Texas. Above all, he wanted to preach; but since he knew few people in Texas, preaching opportunities were scarce.

He returned to Vanderbilt for his senior year and was called as pastor of the Bethel Baptist Church, a rural church in Robertson County. He also worked in the Woodie Barton Goodwill Center. He then went to Southern Baptist Theological Seminary in Louisville, where he received the B.D. degree in 1946. Union University conferred the D.D. degree on him in 1964.

During a trip home while he was a student in Southern Baptist Seminary, Wayne met Lealice Bishop, of Madisonville, Kentucky, a fine arts major at Peabody College. After a whirlwind courtship, they were married on August 24, 1944, and moved into the parsonage at Rogersville, Tennessee, where he was serving as pastor while attending the seminary. They have three children: Rebecca Ann, Katherine Elaine, and William Wayne.

Mr. Dehoney served as pastor at Pineville, Kentucky, and then at Immanuel Baptist Church, Paducah, Kentucky, before going on to the Central Park Baptist Church in Birmingham, Alabama, in 1950. It was during the seven years at Central Park that he first claimed the attention of Southern Baptists with the rapid growth and expansion of that church. He became pastor of the First Baptist Church, Jackson, Tennessee, in 1957, where he stayed until January 1967, when he was called as pastor of the Walnut Street Baptist Church, Louisville.

Wayne Dehoney does not claim to be a theologian, although he is a close student of the Bible and has written several books. He is conversant with developments in the theological field. His major concern has been the "outreach for the unreached." His growing conviction is that man must be reached for God where he is in today's world with the only message which can change him into the kind of person he ought to be.

H. Franklin Paschall
1967-1968

At the 1968 Southern Baptist Convention in Houston vice-president Fred Hubbs was preparing to introduce H. Franklin Paschall for his presidential address when a rather large lady stepped to the podium and started to sing. Mr. Hubbs saw the lady was confused and not on the program. Ushers helped her to a seat on the platform.

That night, Dr. Paschall asked Fred Hubbs what was going through his mind at the interruption. The vice-president replied, "I prayed that if the Lord was ever going to rapture me—now was the time."

Through all of the commotion, Dr. Paschall kept his calm and went on to preside at the Convention where a statement was adopted on racial understanding which made a significant contribution in making the racial issue lose its tension in Southern Baptist churches. Dr. Paschall had already led his own church in adopting a policy of openness to all races.

H. Franklin Paschall was born May 12, 1922, in Hazel, Kentucky. His early education was in a one-room county school, and his "very clear" call to the pastoral ministry came soon after his conversion at the age of fourteen in the Oak Grove Baptist Church. During his first year at Union University, he was called as pastor of a rural church and has been "preaching" ever since.

While in Union, Dr. Paschall not only won a degree, cum laude, but also won the hand of Olga Bailey, a fellow student and also a resident of Hazel. He entered Southern Seminary in 1946 and completed his Th.D. degree in April 1951. He served as pastor of the First Baptist Church, Bowling Green, Kentucky, from 1951 until 1955 when he accepted the call of the First Baptist Church in Nashville, Tennessee. The Paschalls have two daughters, Pamela and Sandra.

W. A. Criswell
1969-1970

Two twelve-year-old boys sat with bowed heads in an old
farm shed near Texline, Texas. Between them was their faithful dog—the victim of a fiendish poisoner.

Slowly, one of the boys rose to his feet. With all of the el-
oquence at his command, he extolled the virtues of the dog,
their companion on many a romp over the plains. Utter contempt was verbally poured on those who would sink so low
as to poison a boy's dog. As the funeral sermon for the dog
continued, tears swelled into the eyes of the lone mourner.
Soon, those tears were rolling down his face to make little
white marks through the dust and dirt on his face.

Thus, W. A. Criswell, pastor of the First Baptist Church of
Dallas, and former president of the Southern Baptist Convention "preached his first sermon."

W. A. Criswell was born on December 19, 1909, at Eldorado,
Oklahoma. His parents were both members of the Baptist
church and W. A. attended his first Sunday School in Oklahoma.
When he was six, the family moved to Texline, Texas; and it
was there, at the age of ten, that he accepted Christ as Savior.

L. S. Hill was the pastor of the Texline Church at the time. Two years later young Criswell felt that God wanted him to be a preacher.

"I do not know what it was that gave me the feeling that I ought to preach," Dr. Criswell said in telling of his experience. "My mother wanted me to be a doctor like her father. I do not remember any special service in the church where the appeal was given for special service, but I had a definite conviction to come in my heart that God wanted me to preach and that feeling has not changed to this day."

When W. A. Criswell was thirteen years old, he was elected president of the B.Y.P.U. in the Texline Church. He attributes much of his early training to the B.Y.P.U., but let him tell the story:

"I was just a country kid and I was literally scared to death when I tried to preside for the first time. We had one B. Y. P. U. in our little church and there were all ages from the youngest to the oldest in our group. I know that the training I received in that B. Y. P. U. did much to stimulate my interest in the affairs of the church and I thank God for the opportunity.

When W. A. was a junior in high school, the Criswells moved into Amarillo so the two boys in the family could attend high school. There, the young preacher entered into all of the school activities and was a member of the debating team. Dr. G. L. Yates was pastor in the First Baptist Church of Amarillo and W. A. was licensed by that church in 1929 just as he was preparing to leave for Baylor University. He was ordained a year later.

Just before he left for Baylor University, Dr. Criswell met the late Dr. George W. Truett for the first time. Dr. Truett went to Amarillo for a revival meeting. The great pastor made a profound influence on the young preacher.

After graduation from Baylor University, W. A. Criswell

went to Louisville, Kentucky, to attend the Southern Baptist Theological Seminary. It was not long before the young Texas preacher was called as pastor at Oakland, Kentucky, a good strong half-time church. He also served as pastor of several other half-time churches. One of these churches was at Mount Washington. The attractive pianist at the Mount Washington Church was Miss Betty Harris. But she was not to be Miss Betty Harris for long. After a fast and furious courtship, which was the talk of the seminary campus, the pianist became Mrs. W. C. Criswell. She joined her husband in continuing her educational training.

Shortly before W. A. Criswell was to receive his doctor's degree from the Seminary in 1937, an associational Brotherhood meeting was planned for Oakland and those on the program included Dr. John L. Hill and B. B. McKinney. Other speakers on the program did not appear and the pastor was asked to fill in for a sermon. When the meeting was over, Dr. Hill gave the young preacher a great deal of encouragement. B. B. McKinney wrote his name and address on a piece of paper, folded the paper, and put it in his billfold. When Dr. Hill returned to Nashville he found a letter from the First Baptist Church of Birmingham, Alabama, on his desk asking about a preacher. He sent Dr. Criswell's name to the committee and a visit was invited. The committee was impressed but the call could not be extended at that time. They asked the young preacher to wait for a few weeks.

Meanwhile, the First Baptist Church of Chickasha in Oklahoma was without a pastor. One of the members was attending Peabody College in Nashville, and since B. B. McKinney had been at the Falls Creek Assembly in Oklahoma for so many years, the Chickasha member visited the Sunday School Board and asked him if he knew of a promising young preacher. Mr. McKinney took out his billfold and the folded piece of paper—and in a few weeks the Criswell family was heading west with all of their earthly possessions.

"To tell the truth, I really wanted to go to Birmingham," Dr. Criswell said with a twinkle in his eye as he recounted the experience, "but Betty and I had made a covenant to go to the first place called after graduation, and when the call came from Chickasha, we felt that God was truly in the call. I wanted to stay in the East, but God called me to the West."

It was while the Criswells were at Chickasha that Mable Ann, their daughter, was born.

After three years at Chickasha, Dr. Criswell was called as pastor of the First Baptist Church of Muskogee; and after three years there he was unanimously called as pastor of the First Baptist Church of Dallas to succeed Dr. Truett.

He was elected as president of the Southern Baptist Convention in Houston in 1968 and presided at New Orleans and Denver.

Carl E. Bates
1971-1972

One of the prized possessions of Carl Bates, pastor of the First Baptist Church of Charlotte, North Carolina, and former president of the Southern Baptist Convention, is a plaque made from a part of a wooden door in the old DeSoto Hotel in New Orleans.

This was not an ordinary door. This was the door to Room 244. The plaque features the shiny brass numerals 244 and the gold-plated key with its identification tag.

Why is this plaque so important?

In 1934 during the depth of the depression, Carl Bates, just out of high school in Liberty, Mississippi, went to New Orleans to look for a job. Work was hard to find; but finally he found a temporary job as a dishwasher and bellhop at the DeSoto Hotel in exchange for board and room. He was assigned to Room 244.

Depressed and uncertain, one night young Carl opened the Bible in his room to read. Out of that experience came a conviction and a call to the gospel ministry.

Carl Bates was born on a farm in Amite County near

Liberty, Mississippi, September 1914, the son of Mr. and Mrs. R. E. Bates. He attended the Amite County High School, and it was before he went back to college in Mississippi that he had the experience in New Orleans.

While Carl was a student in Southern Baptist Seminary, he married Myra Gray of Tupelo, Mississippi, on November 15, 1939. Their daughter, Judy, is married to Joseph W. Stoneham.

Carl Bates served as pastor of rural churches at Habit, Macedonia, and Corydon before accepting the call of the Central Baptist Church in Winchester, Kentucky, after completing his theological work in Southern Seminary in 1941. He served churches in Florida, Texarkana, Amarillo and then accepted the call of the First Baptist Church in Charlotte on July 19, 1959.

At the meeting of the Southern Baptist Convention in Kansas City in 1963, Carl Bates preached the Convention sermon and was nominated as president by Dr. Norris Palmer of Baton Rouge. Although he led all nominees on the first ballot, he asked that his name be withdrawn. Finally in 1970 at the Denver Convention he allowed his name to be presented again; and he was elected. He presided at the sessions at St. Louis and Philadelphia.

Dr. Bates had been honored by Mississippi College, Baylor University, and Wake Forest University with honorary doctorates. He has served as president of both the Texas and North Carolina conventions. He has served on numerous boards. His wife, Myra, has served on the Foreign Mission Board. He counts as his greatest trophy his acceptance by young people who confide in him as pastor and friend.

Owen Cooper
1973-1974

"He didn't come up here to Philadelphia in no watermelon truck. He has held every office there is for a layman to hold in his local church. He doesn't go around talking about church. He's involved. He was in B.Y.P.U. He was in Training Union. He is in Church Training; and if they had voted for Quest, he would be in that."

The speaker was Jerry Clower, the nationally known comedian from Yazoo City, Mississippi.

The place was Philadelphia, Pennsylvania, at the Southern Baptist Convention in 1972.

Jerry's purpose was the nomination of Owen Cooper, a fellow church member from Yazoo City, to be the president of the Southern Baptist Convention, the first layman since Brooks Hays in 1958 and the sixth layman in the history of the Southern Baptist Convention.

Jerry Clower was right. Owen Cooper has served in just about every office in his church. He has been Sunday School teacher and superintendent. He has been Training Union director. He has been a deacon. He has been a lay preacher.

He has been B.S.U. leader. He has been moderator of his association.

Owen Cooper was born in Warren County, Mississippi, on April 19, 1908. He attended Culkin Academy in Warren County, received his B.S. from Mississippi State University in 1929 and his M.A. from the University of Mississippi in 1936.

After a time as a teacher, Cooper joined the Mississippi and Coastal Chemical Corporation, a fertilizer manufacturer, and later became the president. He served here until his retirement in 1974.

On September 2, 1938, Owen Cooper married Elizabeth Thompson of Madison, Georgia; and she has shared his many interests with him.

Owen Cooper has been president of the New Orleans Baptist Seminary trustees, chairman of the Southern Baptist Convention Executive Committee, president of the Mississippi Baptist Convention, vice-president of the Baptist World Alliance, and director of many other organizations. But the responsibility that has given him the greatest pleasure is working on a one-to-one basis to help small churches in some of the pioneer areas of the Southern Baptist Convention or some remote place in the world.

In his closing message to the Convention in Dallas, he said:

"(1) We need to provide more training for more of our ministers. A recent survey indicated that 22 percent of our ministers have a high school education or less; 69 percent have either attended college or completed college or have seminary training; and 36½ percent have completed seminary training.

"(2) We must recognize that the task of winning the world for Christ cannot be done by 'paid' persons alone. Their efforts and their leadership must be supplemented by an increasing number of committee lay people who are willing, able, and eager to share their faith. I believe in a God-called ministry. I believe that God still bestows the 'highest gift,' prophecy, to some and then lays his hands upon them to be his servants and the shepherd of his flocks. But the increasing perplexity of the age in which we live together with the frustration of adults, the trauma of youth, the confusion in our homes, plus the increasing administrative responsibilities of our pastors all make added demands upon the pastor's time.

"(3) Southern Baptists suffer a substantial talent drain. There are pastors leaving the pulpit, denominational administrators gaining secular employment, missionaries resigning, and lay people become involved in a multitude of existing or newly organized groups not related to the Southern Baptist Convention, such as Bible schools, educational institutions, evangelistic, missions, civic, and health organizations.

"We spend thousands of dollars educating ministers; we spend additional thousands of dollars transporting and housing missionaries; we are short of pastors and in need of eight hundred more foreign missionaries and hundreds of additional home missionaries; hence, we can ill afford losses in these categories. This is an appropriate area of concern to all Southern Baptists and should be made an object of continuous consideration.

"(4) There are 100 million people in the Northeast one sixth of this country. Forty-five million of them are unchurched. Embraced in this area is the financial, transportation, governmental, educational, entertainment, and political capital of the world. We should be making an all-out effort to claim more of these people for Christ.

"The North-Central states including Ohio, Indiana, Michigan, Illinois, Wisconsin, and Minnesota are developing a program to double the number of churches and their total work by 1990. The Home Mission Board will be helping. This is a challenge to us all. Perhaps there are individuals, churches, associations, and even state conventions that could find useful ways in which they could get involved in this challenging task.

"(5) We should intensify our teaching and promotion of stewardship not only to provide funds to extend the gospel but to combat secularism and materialism. Christians grow by giving; increase by sharing; and enlarge by dividing. Full cooperation with plans for the 50th Anniversary observance of the Cooperative Program is a worthy goal for each church.

"(6) Southern Baptists should be more cooperative in joint endeavors with other Christian bodies in areas of mutual concern. We can share our knowledge of evangelism without losing enthusiasm; we can share our genius in organization without affecting the organization; and we can share 'in dialogue' our theology without our beliefs being destroyed.

"(7) As individuals, churches, and organizations, Southern Baptists need to appropriate and depend more upon the presence, power, and work of the Holy Spirit. We need more Spirit-filled people, Spirit-filled churches, Spirit-filled agencies, and Spirit-filled meetings. As we become continually led by the Holy Spirit we become effective ministers in the hands of God.

"Southern Baptists should be proud of their heritage. They can look back with satisfaction on reasonable accomplishments, and they can face the challenge of the future with assurance knowing that God is available and that he will hear those who ask and open the door to those who seek. We are not alone in this task. The Holy Spirit is by our side and certainly Christ will return, for surely the King is coming. Let us be ready."

Jaroy Weber
1975-1976

One of the most dramatic moments in Southern Baptist life came at the conclusion of the presidential message of Jaroy Weber on June 10, 1975 , when the replica of the Liberty Bell rang out through the giant convention hall in Miami Beach.

Dr. Weber had just told the story of the man who took his small son back to the community where he had been raised. When they found the old church deserted and abandoned, they started ringing the old bell in the belfry, and the people in the community headed for the church.

As the bell in Miami started to peal, Dr. Weber concluded: "To make a long story short . . . that church is now a thriving, rural church and is in good repair. They have a full-time work. All because a father rang the bell that called people back to a building, and back to a faith, strengthened lives, and strengthened homes."

Jaroy Weber was born in Shirley, Louisiana, on December 27, 1921, the son of Mr. and Mrs. Edward Weber. He grew up at St. Landry, Louisiana, and became exposed to Baptist life early as he went to Acadia and then completed his work at Louisiana College in 1946.

Three things happened in 1939 as he finished Acadia Baptist Academy that changed the life of the young seventeen year old. The first was his marriage to Nettie Wiggins of Beaumont on February 17, and the second was his ordination as a minister by the St. Landry Baptist Church. The third was the call to the Little Cypress Baptist Church and the North Orange Baptist Church of Orange, Texas.

After serving as pastor for ten years at North Orange, he went to First Church, West Monroe, Louisiana. While serving these two churches he also completed work for his degree at Southwestern Baptist Seminary. He was called to the First Baptist Church of Lubbock after serving for five years at the Dauphin Way Church in Mobile, Alabama.

The Webers have three children—Jaroy, Jr., a plastic surgeon in California; Billy, pastor of the Northway Church in Dallas; and Nettie Beth, music director for a church in South Carolina.

Jaroy Weber has emphasized evangelism in all of his pastorates, and his goal for the Southern Baptist Convention has been a greater evangelistic outreach in the nation's Bicentennial year.

"Every great achievement of our denomination has been out of crisis," Weber believes. "We must have confidence that, despite conditions, we will exceed what we have done in the past in evangelism and missions."

These two thrusts represent his heartbeat and goals.

James L. Sullivan
1977-

June 15, 1976 was a dramatic day in Southern Baptist life. As a part of the nation's Bicentennial, Southern Baptists had voted to meet in Norfolk and history-saturated Virginia. The President of the United States, Gerald R. Ford, had spoken in the afternoon as the first president ever to address the Southern Baptist Convention while in office. As registration of messengers was climbing to an all-time high, they could not all be seated in the main meeting place.

Thus, the time for the election of officers had to be postponed so messengers in three different halls—the Scope in Norfolk, nearby Chrysler Hall, and the Dome in Virginia Beach—might vote for the president. Five good men were nominated, and Jesse Fletcher, Knoxville pastor, concluded the nominations by presenting the name of James L. Sullivan. Since the ballots had to be collected from three places it was impossible to report the vote that night, so the drama built. Next morning, the secretary, Fred Kendall, announced that registration stood at 17,986 and James L. Sullivan had been elected as the new president by a clear majority.

James L. Sullivan did not need an introduction to Southern Baptists. He was born in Lawrence County, Mississippi, March 12, 1910, at "the buckle of the Bible belt," as he calls it. The Sullivans were as thick as flies in Sullivan Hollow, Mississippi, and the fact that his father's name was James Washington Sullivan indicated something of his background and patriotic spirit. His mother was Mary Ellen Danpeer before her marriage, and her parents received a grant of land in Mississippi because of the contribution the family had made in the Revolutionary War.

The family called Tylertown home after two years, and young Jim completed high school at the Tylertown High School in 1928 and finished Mississippi College in 1932. He distinguished himself in college not only as a ministerial student, but as a member of the football team that won lasting fame in upsetting Mississippi State University at their homecoming. From Mississippi College he went on to the Southern Baptist Theological Seminary where he received the Th.M. degree in 1935. He has received honorary doctorates from Mississippi College and Campbell College.

Even while serving as Executive Secretary (later President) of the Sunday School Board, 1953-1975, Dr. Sullivan considered himself as a pastor-at-large. Before moving to Nashville with the Sunday School Board, he had served pastorates in Kentucky, Tennessee, Mississippi, and Texas. He came to the Sunday School Board from the pastorate of the First Baptist Church, Abilene, Texas.

At the meeting of the Baptist World Alliance in Stockholm in 1975, Dr. Sullivan was named one of the vice-presidents and also was selected to serve as chairman of the Division of Evangelism and Education.

On October 22, 1935, Jim Sullivan married Velma Scott who had been his boyhood sweetheart. They have three children, Mary Beth (Mrs. Bob Taylor), Martha Lynn (Mrs. James

M. Poarch, Jr.), and James David.

Like J. B. Gambrell, another native Mississippian who served as president of the Convention, James L. Sullivan has a natural store of illustrations from his boyhood and from his early experiences which enable him to translate abstract and difficult concepts into objective and clear understanding. One illustration of this is the title of a book he used to describe Southern Baptist unity as a *Rope of Sand with Strength of Steel.*

"The most important organizational unit of the denomination is the local church," Dr. Sullivan wrote. "Although the units of organization called associations, statewide bodies usually called state conventions, and the nationwide Southern Baptist Convention have their places, we cannot overemphasize the importance of a local congregation. The local church is more vital than all other areas combined. It is at the local level that 'the water hits the wheel.' If work is not done there, it is not done anywhere. If it is done well there, its successes become the denomination's strength."

Dr. Sullivan believes that in any organization advance follows a sort of rhythm. In a *Rope of Sand with Strength of Steel* he said, "The rhythm of growth in a denomination like ours is like a ship plowing a rough sea. The waves are beating against it, first on the right side and then on the left. The ship's captain must give attention to these pressures, but the thrust of the ship is forward. The captain must maintain balance so that the ship is not capsized by the waves sweeping it from the sides. Progress is made not by the side sweeps that tilt the ship, but from the forward thrust that moves it toward its destination.

"Convention leaders have learned to deal with the pressures of extremism that sweep through the country and affect every religious body, first from the right and then from the left. One time it is from the ultraconservatives, and another time from the ultraliberals. Neither can prevail, nor should they." Dr. Sullivan continued, "A ship has a certain amount of tolerance. The captain must take into account winds that blow, but never can he allow the ship to be swept off course in either direction or the whole cargo is lost."

When Dr. Sullivan wrote these words, he did not know that one day he would be called on to be the captain of the ship. Southern Baptists can look to him with the assurance that he will follow the guidance of the Holy Spirit.